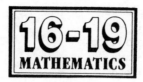

16-19
MATHEMATICS

Differential equations

The School Mathematics Project

REFERENCE

CAMBRIDGE
UNIVERSITY PRESS

Main authors Stan Dolan
Mike Leach
Tim Lewis
Richard Peacock
Jeff Searle
Phil Wood

Team leader Jeff Searle

Project director Stan Dolan

The authors would like to give special thanks to Ann White for her help in preparing this book for publication.

Drawings by Bunny Graphics

The publishers would like to thank Foto Leidmann/ZEFA for permission to reproduce the photograph on page 38.

Published by the Press Syndicate of the University of Cambridge
The Pitt Building, Trumpington Street, Cambridge CB2 1RP
40 West 20th Street, New York, NY 10011-4211, USA
10 Stamford Road, Oakleigh, Melbourne 3166, Australia

First published 1992
Reprinted 1994

Produced by 16-19 Mathematics, Southampton

Printed in Great Britain by Athenæum Press Ltd, Newcastle upon Tyne

ISBN 0 521 42649 9 paperback

Contents

1 Review

1.1 The order of a differential equation

The idea of a differential equation has already been met in *Mathematical methods*.

> (a) How do differential equations arise?
>
> (b) Why is the solution of differential equations important?
>
> (c) What methods of solution are available?

You know that gradient functions are obtained by the process known as differentiation.

For example,

$$y = x^3 - 5x^2 - 4x + 20$$

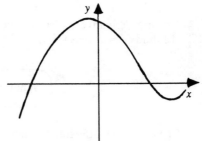

$$\frac{dy}{dx} = 3x^2 - 10x - 4$$

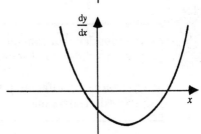

The process can be repeated to find the gradient function of the gradient function:

$$\frac{d^2y}{dx^2} = 6x - 10$$

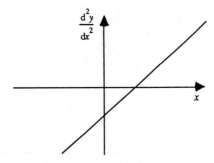

The notation $\frac{d^2y}{dx^2}$ follows logically from the use of $\frac{d}{dx}$ to mean 'differentiate with respect to x', i.e. $\frac{d}{dx}\left(\frac{dy}{dx}\right) = \frac{d^2y}{dx^2}$.

1

If $y = x^3 - 5x^2 - 4x + 20$, find:

(a) $\dfrac{d^3 y}{dx^3}$ (b) $\dfrac{d^4 y}{dx^4}$

$\dfrac{d^2 y}{dx^2}$, $\dfrac{d^3 y}{dx^3}$ and so on, are called **higher derivatives.**

$\dfrac{d^2 y}{dx^2}$ is called the second derivative or the derivative of **order 2.**

$\dfrac{d^n y}{dx^n}$ is called the nth derivative or the derivative of order n.

Sometimes it is more convenient to use function notation to express higher derivatives. The order of the derivative using function notation is represented by dashes and by numbers in brackets. For example, suppose $f(t) = 3 \sin 2t$.

The first derivative is $f'(t) = 6 \cos 2t$, the second derivative is $f''(t) = -12 \sin 2t$ and the third derivative is $f^{(3)}(t) = -24 \cos 2t$.

What is $f^{(4)}(t)$ if $f(t) = 3 \sin 2t$?

The order of a differential equation is defined as follows.

Any equation that contains a derivative or a number of derivatives is called a differential equation.

The order of a differential equation is equal to the order of the highest derivative that appears in the equation.

(a) $\dfrac{dy}{dx} = 2x - 3$

(b) $\dfrac{d^2 x}{dt^2} = 3x^2 - 2x + 1$

(c) $\dfrac{d^2 \theta}{dt^2} = -w^2 \theta$

(d) $\dfrac{d^2 r}{ds^2} = -r \dfrac{dr}{ds}$

(e) $\dfrac{d^3 y}{dx^3} - 2 \dfrac{d^2 y}{dx^2} = 4$

(f) $\dfrac{d^3 x}{dt^3} = \cos 2t \ e^x$

What is the order of each of the differential equations above?

Examples involving first and second derivatives are common in mechanics problems. If, for example, x represents the displacement of a particle from a fixed point, then $\frac{dx}{dt}$ represents its velocity and $\frac{d^2x}{dt^2}$ its acceleration.

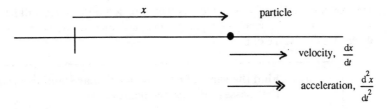

Example 1

A particle moves on the x-axis in such a way that its displacement x metres, at time t seconds, is

$$x = -3 + 3t - 4t^2 + \frac{4}{3}t^3$$

(a)   Find the displacement, velocity and acceleration of the particle after one second.

(b)   Show that the particle is at rest twice during the first two seconds of its motion.

(c)   Describe the motion of the particle after two seconds.

Solution

(a)   Displacement $x = -3 + 3t - 4t^2 + \frac{4}{3}t^3$

   Velocity $\frac{dx}{dt} = 3 - 8t + 4t^2$

   Acceleration $\frac{d^2x}{dt^2} = -8 + 8t$

   When $t = 1$, $x = -2\frac{2}{3}$, $\frac{dx}{dt} = -1$ and $\frac{d^2x}{dt^2} = 0$

   The particle is $2\frac{2}{3}$ m to the left of the origin and moving away at 1 ms⁻¹, having instantaneously reached its maximum speed.

(b) $\frac{dx}{dt} = 3 - 8t + 4t^2 = (1 - 2t)(3 - 2t)$

   The particle is at rest when $(1 - 2t)(3 - 2t) = 0 \Rightarrow t = \frac{1}{2}$ or $1\frac{1}{2}$.

(c)   When $t = 2$, $x = -2\frac{1}{3}$, $\frac{dx}{dt} = 3$ and $\frac{d^2x}{dt^2} = 8$.

   The particle is $2\frac{1}{3}$ m to the left of the origin, moving towards it at 3 ms⁻¹ and accelerating rapidly. It will pass the origin and continue to accelerate away from it.

3

1.2 Solution by inspection

Occasionally, it is possible to 'look' at a differential equation and 'see' a solution.

For example, if $\frac{dy}{dx} = 3x^2 + 1$, then its family of solution curves will have equations $y = x^3 + x + c.$ Specifying a point that a particular solution curve must pass through determines the value of c.

> (a) **Find the value of c for the particular solution curve that passes through the point (1, 3).**
>
> (b) **Sketch the family of solution curves.**

Exercise 1

1. For the following differential equations, find, by inspection, equations for the families of solution curves.

    (a) $\frac{dy}{dx} = 2x - 3$ (b) $\frac{dy}{dx} = 2x^{-3}$

    (c) $\frac{ds}{dt} = \frac{1}{t^2}$ (d) $\frac{dx}{dt} = 2\cos 2t$

    (e) $x^2 \frac{dy}{dx} = 2$ (f) $\frac{ds}{dt} = 3e^t$

    (g) $\frac{dy}{dx} = \frac{1}{\sqrt{x}}$ (h) $\frac{d^2y}{dx^2} = 3x^2$

    (i) $\frac{d^2s}{dt^2} = \sin t$ (j) $\frac{d^2x}{dt^2} = \sin 2t$

2. If $\frac{dy}{dx} = x^2 - 2,$ find the solution curves that pass through:

    (a) (3, 5)   (b) (5, 3)

3. If $\frac{dx}{dt} = \cos 3t$, find the solution curves that pass through:

    (a) (0, 0)   (b) $(\frac{\pi}{6}, 1)$

4. If $\frac{d^2y}{dx^2} = 3x^2 - 2x - 1$, find the solution curve that passes through (0, 2) and (4, 4).

1.3　A numerical step-by-step method

For a first order differential equation, the gradient function gives the gradient of the tangent at any point on the curve, and this is used for the step-by-step method when finding a solution curve.

From any starting point, the gradient function tells you in which direction to proceed in order to build up a solution.

Example 2

Use a numerical method to find the solution curve for $\frac{dy}{dx} = 3x^2 + 1$, which passes through (1, 3).

Solution

At (1, 3) the gradient is 4.

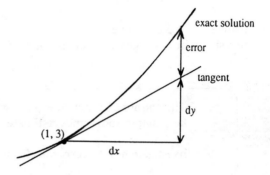

You must first decide the step size, for example $dx = 0.1$, and then use the differential equation to estimate the corresponding step, dy, in y. The point $(x + dx, y + dy)$ is only an estimate for a point on the curve because you have followed the tangent rather than the curve itself.

The solution curve is built up by repeating the process over and over again, taking the latest estimated point as the new starting point each time.

The numerical solution can be shown in a table, although the stage-by-stage numerical details are often held in the memory of a programmable calculator or computer.

x	y	$\frac{dy}{dx}$	dx	dy	$x + dx$	$y + dy$
1	3	4	0.1	0.4	1.1	3.4
1.1	3.4	4.63	0.1	0.463	1.2	3.863
1.2	3.863					

> **(a)** Continue the table to obtain an estimate of y when $x = 1.5$.
>
> **(b)** Use a suitable program to check your results for the table above, and extend it to $x = 2.0$.
>
> Also (if possible) check your results using a solution sketching program.

For $\frac{dy}{dx} = 3x^2 + 1$, you can investigate the size of the error in the numerical solution since the exact solution can be obtained by inspection.

The equation of the solution curve through $(1, 3)$ is:

$$y = x^3 + x + 1$$

Putting $x = 1.5$ gives an exact value of $y = 5.875$. The step-by-step method, with a step size of $dx = 0.1$, gives an estimate of $y = 5.690$ when $x = 1.5$. The absolute error is 0.185.

> **(a)** With the aid of a sketch, explain why the step-by-step method in the example above underestimates the actual value.
>
> **(b)** Investigate how the error is affected by varying the step size.

The accuracy of a numerical solution can be improved by taking smaller steps, but this involves many more calculations.

TASKSHEET 1 – *Numerical solutions*

The accuracy of a numerical solution depends not only on the size of the step but also on the rate at which the gradient is changing. In a domain where the gradient is changing rapidly, large errors will occur unless the step is very small.

Methods which are more sophisticated than the step-by-step method have been developed, and are usually much more efficient. Often, when solving a differential equation numerically, you will not know the exact solution and so cannot carry out a precise error analysis. However, you need to be confident that any numerical solution is reasonably accurate.

> **The real power of a numerical method is that it can be applied to calculate a solution however complicated the gradient function might be.**

There are a number of computer programs which not only calculate solutions to differential equations, but also allow sketches of the solution curves to be obtained very easily. You should make use of such a program to check your answers in the following exercise.

Exercise 2

1. (a) Find a numerical solution of $\frac{dy}{dx} = x + y$ for $-3 \leq x \leq 3$, starting at $(-3, 2)$ and using a step size of 0.5.

   (b) Repeat part (a) for the starting points $(-3, 2.25)$, $(-3, 2.05)$, $(-3, 1.95)$ and $(-3, 1.75)$.

   (c) Sketch the solution curve that passes through $(-3, 2)$ by plotting your numerical solution.

      Sketch the other members of the family of solution curves on the same axes.

   (d) Conjecture what happens to the family of solution curves for large negative x.

2. The motion of a parachutist after her parachute has opened is modelled by the differential equation $\frac{dv}{dt} = 10 - 0.1v^2$.

   If $v = 15\,\mathrm{ms}^{-1}$ when the parachute opens, calculate the velocity after 2 seconds, using a time step of 0.2 second. Explain what is happening physically.

3. A market researcher proposes the model $\frac{dn}{dp} = -\frac{10^6}{p^3}$ to describe how demand for a certain product varies with its price, where n is the number of articles sold per week at a price £p.

   If a price of £10 gives weekly sales of 5000 articles, estimate how many will be sold if the price is increased to £12.

After working through this chapter you should:

1. know what is meant by a higher derivative and the order of a differential equation;

2. have revised how to obtain solutions by inspection where appropriate;

3. have revised how to calculate approximate solutions by a step-by-step method for first order equations;

4. appreciate that a curve sketched using a numerical solution is an approximation to one member of a family of solution curves;

5. have developed some appreciation of the errors involved in numerical solutions.

Numerical solutions

1. (a) Obtain numerical solutions to $\frac{dy}{dx} = x^3 + 1$ for $0 \leq x \leq 1$, starting at $(0, 0)$ and using step sizes of

   (i) 0.2   (ii) 0.1   (iii) 0.05

   (b) Obtain the exact solution by inspection. Quantify and comment on any improvement in accuracy as the step size gets smaller.

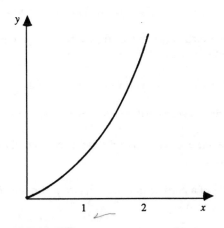

   (c) Repeat (a) and (b) for $1 \leq x \leq 2$, starting at $(1, 1.25)$. Comment on how the domain affects the accuracy.

2. (a) Obtain numerical solutions to $\frac{dh}{dt} = 2 \sin 3t$, for $\frac{\pi}{12} \leq t \leq \frac{\pi}{4}$, starting at $(\frac{\pi}{12}, -\frac{\sqrt{2}}{3})$ and using step sizes of

   (i) $\frac{\pi}{24}$ (ii) $\frac{\pi}{48}$

   (b) Obtain the exact solution by inspection. Quantify and comment on any improvement in accuracy as the step size gets smaller.

   (c) Repeat (a) and (b) for $-\frac{\pi}{12} \leq t \leq \frac{\pi}{12}$, starting at $(-\frac{\pi}{12}, -\frac{\sqrt{2}}{3})$. Comment on how the domain affects the accuracy.

1. (a) What are the fourth derivatives of   (i) $y = x^5$ (ii) $y = \sin x$?

    (b) Find the higher derivatives of   (i) $y = x^5$ (ii) $y = \sin x$.

2. If $y = \sin wx$, show that $\dfrac{d^2y}{dx^2} = -w^2y$.

3. (a) If $f(x) = x^2 - 1$, show that $f'(x) - 3x\,f(x) = 5x - 3x^3$.

    (b) If $g(t) = e^{-2t}$, show that $g''(t) + 3g'(t) + 2g(t) = 0$.

4. A ball is thrown vertically upwards from a height of 2 metres. After t seconds, its height h metres is given by $h = 2 + 8t - 5t^2$.

    (a) Find the velocity of the ball when it is released.

    (b) At what time does the ball reach its maximum height? What is this height?

    (c) Show that the acceleration of the ball is constant throughout its motion. Comment on its value.

5. The coordinates of a particle moving in a circle of radius 3 metres are given by $x = 3 \cos 2t$, $y = 3 \sin 2t$.

    (a) Find the components of the velocity, $\dfrac{dx}{dt}$ and $\dfrac{dy}{dt}$, and those of the acceleration, $\dfrac{d^2x}{dt^2}$ and $\dfrac{d^2y}{dt^2}$, after 1 and 2 seconds.

    (b) Show that $\dfrac{dx}{dt} = -2y$ and $\dfrac{d^2x}{dt^2} = -4x$ at any time t.

    (c) Express $\dfrac{dy}{dt}$ and $\dfrac{d^2y}{dt^2}$ in terms of x and y.

    (d) Interpret the results of (b) and (c) in terms of the motion of the particle.

6. (a) Find solutions of $\dfrac{dy}{dx} = xy - 1$ for $-2 \le x \le 2$, using a step size of 0.2, and starting at the following points:

    (i) $(-2, 75)$ (ii) $(-2, 50)$ (iii) $(-2, 25)$

    (iv) $(-2, 0)$ (v) $(-2, -25)$ (vi) $(-2, -50)$

    (b) Sketch the family of solution curves.

    (c) Repeat (a) for a step size of 0.5. Comment on, and explain, what happens.

2 Numerical solutions

2.1 Parametric equations

You have seen how the step-by-step method can be applied to calculate a solution to an equation of the form $\frac{dy}{dx} = f(x, y)$. The method can be extended to cases where x and y and their derivatives are expressed in terms of a parameter t.

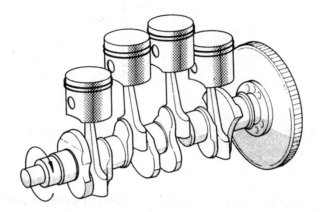

Consider a particular situation where the velocity of the point of connection (x, y) of a conrod to a rotating shaft is given by the equations:

$$\frac{dx}{dt} = 4 \cos t - 3 \sin t$$

$$\frac{dy}{dt} = -3 \cos t - 4 \sin t$$

Starting from the point $(x, y, t) = (3, 4, 0)$, you could choose a small step of $dt = 0.2$ and draw up tables to estimate the values of x and of y at any time.

t	x	y	dt	dx	dy
0	3.0	4.0	0.2	0.8	−0.6
0.2	3.8	3.4	0.2	0.66	−0.75
0.4	4.46	2.65	0.2	0.50	−0.86
0.6	4.97	1.79	0.2	0.32	
0.8					
1.0					

> **Complete the table to obtain an estimate of the position of the point of connection when $t = 1.0$.**

11

To illustrate the numerical solution, the values of x and y can be plotted separately against the corresponding value of t.

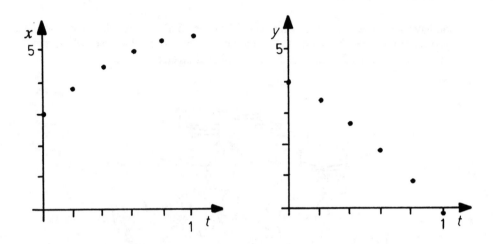

Alternatively, you could plot a graph of y against x or a three-dimensional (x, y, t) diagram.

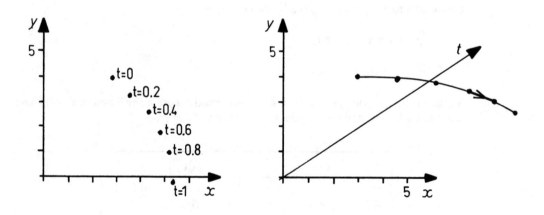

The three-dimensional diagram is useful in illustrating the connection between the numerical solution and the exact solution. Each step follows the tangent to the solution curve through that point. Provided that the graph of the exact solution is locally straight, smaller steps will give a closer approximation to the actual curve.

2.2　Simultaneous linear equations

The equations considered in the previous section,

$$\frac{dx}{dt} = 4 \cos t - 3 \sin t$$

$$\frac{dy}{dt} = -3 \cos t - 4 \sin t$$

can be solved analytically.

(a)　**If $x = 3$ and $y = 4$ when $t = 0$, find the exact solution of these two differential equations.**

(b)　**What is the shape of a graph of y against x?**

The importance of the numerical step-by-step method is that it can be applied even when the equations cannot be solved by an exact method. An example of its use for simultaneous differential equations is given in the next discussion point.

In a chemical reaction involving only butane and methane, the rate at which butane changes into methane depends on the quantity of each present.

Under certain physical conditions, the rates of change are given by

$$\frac{dx}{dt} = -0.2x + 0.7y \quad \text{and} \quad \frac{dy}{dt} = 0.2x - 0.7y$$

where x and y, respectively, denote the overall percentages of butane and methane in the mixture after time t minutes.

(a)　**Write a program to estimate the percentages of butane and methane after 3 minutes if there are equal quantities of each when the reaction starts.**

(b)　**Explain why**

　　(i)　$x + y = 100$　　　**(ii)　$\dfrac{dy}{dt} = -\dfrac{dx}{dt}$**

A simple program enables results to be calculated easily to any reasonable degree of accuracy. The effects of changing the length of step or varying the initial conditions or values of constants can also be readily investigated. Use a program for a computer or programmable calculator to solve the problems on Tasksheet 1.

TASKSHEET 1 – *Stereo tuners*

The step-by-step method can be used to solve two first order differential equations of general form

$$\frac{dx}{dz} = f(x, y, z)$$

$$\frac{dy}{dz} = g(x, y, z)$$

Exercise 1

1. For $0 \le t \le 5$ and using a step of $dt = 0.5$, obtain numerical solutions of the simultaneous equations $\frac{dx}{dt} = -0.2x + 0.7y$, $\frac{dy}{dt} = 0.2x - 0.7y$ which pass through the following points when $t = 0$:

   (a) (70, 30)   (b) (90, 10)   (c) (10, 90)

   Conjecture what happens for $t > 5$, for any specified starting point.

2. Suppose $\frac{dx}{dt} = y$ and $\frac{dy}{dt} = -x$, where $x = 3$ and $y = 4$ when $t = 0$.

   (a) Using a step of $dt = 0.2$, obtain a numerical solution for $0 \le t \le 1$.

   (b) The exact solution is the same as that for the differential equations

   $$\frac{dx}{dt} = 4 \cos t - 3 \sin t$$

   $$\frac{dy}{dt} = -3 \cos t - 4 \sin t$$

   Explain why and comment on the accuracy of your numerical solution.

3. The current i and charge q in a circuit are given by

   $$\frac{di}{dt} = 5.3 - 4.5i - 1.2q \text{ and } \frac{dq}{dt} = i$$

   Initially $i = q = 0$.

   Obtain and sketch solution sets (t, i) and (t, q) for $0 \le t \le 5$, using steps of

   (a) $dt = 0.5$ and (b) $dt = 0.1$

4E. In a chemical reaction with three substances u, v, w,

   $$\frac{du}{dt} = u - v, \quad \frac{dv}{dt} = v - u, \quad \frac{dw}{dt} = u + v$$

   Initially, $u = 110$, $v = 90$ and $w = 100$. Use a step of $dt = 0.1$ to sketch the (t, u), (t, v) and (t, w) curves for $0 \le t \le 1$. Estimate the quantity (u, v, w) when $t = 1$ and explain your results.

2.3   Second order linear equations

The second derivative is needed for many mathematical models. For example:

- $\dfrac{d^2y}{dt^2} = -ky$ is the equation of simple harmonic motion.

- $m\dfrac{d^2x}{dt^2} = mg - k\dfrac{dx}{dt}$ is the equation of motion for a body falling under gravity with air resistance proportional to the speed of the body.

- $\dfrac{d^2q}{dt^2} + R\dfrac{dq}{dt} + \dfrac{q}{C} = V$ models the flow of current in radio circuits.

This section introduces a **numerical** method of solving such equations, given appropriate initial conditions. First, consider a simple case such as

$$\frac{d^2y}{dt^2} = -10$$

which could represent the free fall of a body under gravity.

The velocity, $v = \dfrac{dy}{dt}$, then satisfies the equation

$$\frac{dv}{dt} = -10$$

which can be solved by inspection.

> **For the differential equation $\dfrac{d^2y}{dt^2} = -10$, suppose $y = 7$**
>
> **and $\dfrac{dy}{dt} = 3$ when $t = 0$. Find y when $t = 4$.**

For an equation such as

$$\frac{d^2x}{dt^2} = -x,$$

you can still replace $\dfrac{dx}{dt}$ by v. This produces the equation $\dfrac{dv}{dt} = -x$.

> **Why can this equation not be solved by inspection?**

Although the solution is not so straightforward in this case, the two simultaneous equations

$$\frac{dv}{dt} = -x \quad \text{and} \quad \frac{dx}{dt} = v$$

can be solved as in the previous section.

TASKSHEET 2 – *Second derivatives*

15

Suppose an object moves in a straight line under the action of a force of attraction to a fixed point, the force being proportional to the distance from that point. Suppose further that the object experiences air resistance which is proportional to its speed. Then its motion can be modelled by a differential equation of the form

$$a\,\frac{d^2x}{dt^2} + b\,\frac{dx}{dt} + cx = 0$$

> **Explain each term in this expression and show why the equation of motion has this form.**

Applications of this type of differential equation include the motion of an object attached to an oscillating spring and the proposed, gravity-powered, underground link between New York and Washington.

Example 1

For the differential equation

$$\frac{d^2y}{dx^2} + 2\,\frac{dy}{dx} + 5y = 0$$

estimate the values of y for $0 \le x \le 3$ using a step size of $dx = 0.5$, given that $y = 3$ and $\frac{dy}{dx} = 4$ when $x = 0$.

Solution

Let $\frac{dy}{dx} = v$, then $\frac{dv}{dx} = -2v - 5y$

For a step size of $dx = 0.5$:

x	y	v	dx	dy	dv
0	3	4	0.5	2	−11.5
0.5	5	−7.5	0.5	−3.75	−5
1	1.25	−12.5	0.5	−6.25	9.38
1.5	−5	−3.13	0.5	−1.56	15.63
2	−6.56	12.5	0.5	6.25	3.91
2.5	−0.31	16.41	0.5	8.20	−15.63
3	7.89	0.78			

The results above are inaccurate because of the large step size but they do reveal the oscillatory nature of the motion.

For the example above, greater accuracy can be achieved by using a much smaller step size or by solving the differential equation symbolically. An exact method is given in Chapter 4.

Exercise 2

In each of the following questions, you will need to choose an appropriate step length.

1. (a) Solve $\dfrac{d^2y}{dx^2} + 9y = 4$, starting with $x = 5$ and $\dfrac{dy}{dx} = 1$ at $y = 0$.

   (b) Sketch the (x, y) solution for $5 \le x \le 10$.

2. The position, x metres, of the front of a compression wave at time t seconds satisfies the equation

$$\frac{d^2x}{dt^2} + 0.8\,\frac{dx}{dt} - 3.2x = 1$$

   If $x = 2$ and $\dfrac{dx}{dt} = 0$ when $t = 0$, estimate the speed of the front of the wave when $t = 3$.

3. The charge q coulombs in a circuit at time t seconds satisfies the equation

$$\frac{d^2q}{dt^2} + 9.4\,\frac{dq}{dt} + 5.4q = 7.3$$

   Estimate the current $i = \dfrac{dq}{dt}$ when $t = 2$, given that $q = i = 0$ when $t = 0$.

4E. A surface is given by $\dfrac{dz}{dy} = x$, $\dfrac{dy}{dx} = z^2$.

   (a) Starting at the point $(1, 1, 1)$ and using a step of $dy = 0.5$, obtain a sketch of the surface in each of the (x, y), (x, z) and (y, z) planes for $1 \le y \le 5$.

   (b) Try to repeat part (a) with $dx = 0.5$ for $1 \le x \le 5$. What problem do you encounter?

5E. The variables x and t satisfy the differential equation

$$\frac{d^3x}{dt^3} - 2\,\frac{d^2x}{dt^2} = 3$$

   Given that $x = 0$, $\dfrac{dx}{dt} = 0$ and $\dfrac{d^2x}{dt^2} = 5$ when $t = 0$, estimate x and $\dfrac{dx}{dt}$ when $t = 5$.

After working through this chapter you should:

1.   be able to obtain a numerical solution to a set of two, or more, simultaneous differential equations of first order;

2.   be able to obtain a numerical solution to a second, or higher, order linear differential equation by replacing it by two, or more, simultaneous linear differential equations of first order;

3.   appreciate that the accuracy and validity of a numerical solution depends on both the number of steps and the size of each step.

Stereo tuners

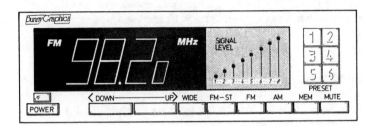

At the heart of a stereo tuner there is a small circuit with inductance L henries, capacitance C farads and resistance R ohms. To tune in to a chosen radio station, the capacitance C is changed by turning the tuning button. The current i amps and charge q coulombs are related to the voltage V volts by the differential equations

$$\frac{di}{dt} = \frac{V}{L} - \left(\frac{R}{L}\right)i - \frac{q}{LC} \text{ and } \frac{dq}{dt} = i$$

1. Suppose $V = 6$, $L = 2$, $R = 8$ and $C = 5$ and suppose that $t = i = q = 0$ initially.

    Complete the table below, using a time interval of $dt = 0.2$, to estimate the current in the circuit after 1 minute.

t	i	q	dt	di	dq
0	0	0	0.2	0.6	0
0.2	0.6	0	0.2	0.12	0.12
0.4					
0.6					
0.8					
1.0					

2. (a) Repeat question 1 with reduced step lengths and with extended times. Make a general statement about the behaviour of the current and the charge.

    (b) Repeat part (a) with different initial conditions.

3. In practice, the voltage is usually not constant, but varies. Discover how the current and charge behave if $V = 6 \cos t$, the other values being unchanged.

Second derivatives

1. (a) Using a step of $dt = 1$, obtain a numerical solution of the following simultaneous equations when $t = 5$, given that $x = 10$ and $v = 4$ when $t = 0$.

$$\frac{dv}{dt} = -x \text{ and } \frac{dx}{dt} = v$$

(b) Sketch the (t, x) and (t, v) solution curves for $0 \le t \le 5$.

(c) Improve your results for part (a), by using a step of $dt = 0.1$

(d) Describe a real context for which the model $\frac{d^2x}{dt^2} = -x$ is appropriate.

In the same way, third order equations can be solved by first expressing them as three first order equations. Indeed, a linear equation of any order can be tackled by this process.

2E. (a) $\frac{d^3x}{dt^3} + 6\frac{d^2x}{dt^2} + 11\frac{dx}{dt} + 6x = 2t$ can be rewritten as:

$$\frac{dx}{dt} = v, \quad \frac{dv}{dt} = y, \quad \frac{dy}{dt} + 6y + 11v + 6x = 2t$$

Starting with $x = \frac{dx}{dt} = \frac{d^2x}{dt^2} = 2$ when $t = 0$, take steps of $dt = 0.5$ to estimate the

value of x when $t = 4$. Sketch the (t, x) solution curve.

(b) Write $\frac{d^3x}{dt^3} + 3t\frac{d^2x}{dt^2} - 5t^2\frac{dx}{dt} + 7x = e^t$

in the form of three simultaneous linear differential equations.

Given that $x = 4$, $\frac{dx}{dt} = 2$ and $\frac{d^2x}{dt^2} = 1$ when $t = 1$, use a step of $dt = 0.1$ to estimate

the values of x, $\frac{dx}{dt}$ and $\frac{d^2x}{dt^2}$ when $t = 2$.

Tutorial sheet

1. The current and charge in a circuit are related by the equations

$$\frac{di}{dt} = 3 - 4i - \frac{q}{2} \text{ and } \frac{dq}{dt} = i$$

Initially, $t = i = q = 0$. Estimate the current i amps and charge q coulombs after 1 second and determine how these quantities behave over extended times.

2. The distance y of a satellite falling towards Earth satisfies the equation

$$\frac{d^2y}{dt^2} = 2\frac{dy}{dt} - \frac{5000}{y^2}$$

Initially $y = 100$ and $\frac{dy}{dt} = 0$.

Estimate the distance y and speed $\frac{dy}{dt}$ when $t = 3$.

3. The velocity of a missile, in metres per second, is given by

$$\frac{dx}{dt} = 4t, \quad \frac{dy}{dt} = 6t, \quad \frac{dz}{dt} = 8 \sin 0.2t$$

(a) Starting from the point $(0, 0, 100)$, take four steps with $dt = 0.5$ to estimate the missile's position after 2 seconds.

(b) Sketch its path in each of the coordinate planes for $0 \le t \le 10$.

4E. A charged particle moves so that its position is given by

$$\frac{dx}{dt} = \frac{x}{y}, \quad \frac{dy}{dt} = \frac{y}{z}, \quad \frac{dz}{dt} = \frac{z}{x}$$

(a) Starting from the point $(1, 1, 1)$, take six steps with $dt = 0.5$ to estimate the particle's position when $t = 3$.

(b) Sketch its path on a diagram with three-dimensional axes.

5E. The original equations used by Lorentz in the development of what is now known as **chaos theory** were:

$$\frac{dx}{dt} = 10 \, (y - x), \quad \frac{dy}{dt} = xz + 28x - y, \quad \frac{dz}{dt} = xy - \frac{8}{3}z$$

Solve these equations, starting with $x = y = z = 1$. Comment on your results.

3   *First order equations*

3.1   Separable variables

Numerical techniques for the solution of differential equations have developed rapidly alongside the development of computers and calculators. With appropriate programs it is usually possible to produce solutions quickly and to any desired degree of accuracy.

However, it is useful to find exact (analytic) solutions when possible because there are limitations to numerical methods.

- Each case is looked at individually. A new member of the family of solution curves is obtained for each set of initial conditions.

- It is not always apparent which function the solution sketcher is sketching.

Consider, for example, the family of solution curves of $\dfrac{dy}{dx} = -\dfrac{x}{y}$.

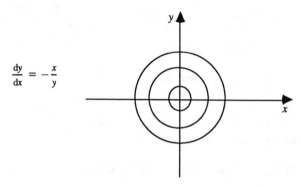

$$\frac{dy}{dx} = -\frac{x}{y}$$

The family of solution curves **looks like** a set of concentric circles or ellipses. To check the precise nature of the family, it is necessary to use calculus techniques to establish a connection between the equation of a circle centred on the origin and the differential equation $\dfrac{dy}{dx} = -\dfrac{x}{y}$.

(a)   Explain why any circle, centre the origin, has an equation of the form $x^2 + y^2 = c$.

(b)   From the equation $x^2 + y^2 = c$, use implicit differentiation to obtain $\dfrac{dy}{dx} = -\dfrac{x}{y}$.

(c)   Reverse the process in (b) to show how $x^2 + y^2 = c$ can be obtained from $\dfrac{dy}{dx} = -\dfrac{x}{y}$.

> If a differential equation can be put in the form $g(y)\dfrac{dy}{dx} = f(x)$
> then the solution can be obtained from
>
> $$\int g(y)\, dy = \int f(x)\, dx$$
>
> This procedure is known as the method of separable variables.

Example 1

(a) Solve the differential equation $\dfrac{dy}{dx} = \dfrac{1}{2y}$.

(b) Sketch the family of solution curves and find the equation of the particular solution through $(1, 2)$.

Solution

(a)
$$2y\, dy = dx$$
$$\Rightarrow \int 2y\, dy = \int dx$$
$$\Rightarrow \quad y^2 = x + c$$

As c can take any value, $y^2 = x + c$ represents the whole family of solution curves. A numerical solution gives only one member of the family.

(b)

$$y^2 = x + c$$
$$4 = 1 + c \quad \text{at } (1, 2)$$
$$\Rightarrow c = 3$$

The particular solution has equation $y^2 = x + 3$.

> **Show that the method of separable variables can be used for**
>
> (a) $\dfrac{dy}{dx} = y^2 x$ and   (b) $\dfrac{dy}{dx} = y^2 x + x$,
>
> **but not for** (c) $\dfrac{dy}{dx} = y^2 x + 1$.

An advantage of obtaining a symbolic solution is that a general solution is often easy to manipulate. In Example 2, a symbolic solution makes it easy to study a particular case of special interest.

Example 2

A stone, falling vertically, is subject to air resistance proportional to its velocity, so that its motion can be modelled by Newton's equation as

$$m \frac{dv}{dt} = mg - mv$$

Find a general expression for v in terms of t.

Solution

Taking g as $10\,\text{ms}^{-2}$, the differential equation can be written

$$\frac{dv}{dt} = 10 - v$$

$$\Rightarrow \int \frac{dv}{10 - v} = \int dt$$

$$\Rightarrow -\ln(10 - v) = t + c$$

$$\Rightarrow 10 - v = e^{-t-c}$$

$$\Rightarrow 10 - v = Ae^{-t}$$

$$\Rightarrow v = 10 - Ae^{-t}$$

(a)   **What is the significance of letting $t \to +\infty$ in the general solution?**

(b)   **What determines the value of A that would be used in a particular solution?**

(c)   **Differentiate $v = 10 - Ae^{-t}$ and eliminate A by combining the equations for v and $\frac{dv}{dt}$. Hence check that $v = 10 - Ae^{-t}$ is a general solution of the differential equation.**

Exercise 1

1.   Solve the differential equations:

(a) $\dfrac{dy}{dx} = y^2$

(b) $\dfrac{dy}{dx} = y$

(c) $\dfrac{dy}{dx} = 3y$

(d) $x^2 \dfrac{dy}{dx} - y + 1 = 0$

24

2. For the differential equation $\frac{dy}{dx} = -2xy$

   (a) find the general solution;

   (b) find the particular solution which passes through the point (0, 4).

3. Which of the following differential equations can be solved by the method of separable variables? Solve those which can.

   (a) $\frac{dy}{dx} = 7 - 5y$

   (b) $\frac{dy}{dx} = xy + 4$

   (c) $x + y\frac{dy}{dx} = 10$

   (d) $\frac{dy}{dx} = \sqrt{xy}$

4. The potential, V volts, at a distance r from the common centre of two spherical conductors of radii 5 cm and 3 cm respectively, is given by

   $$r^2\frac{dV}{dr} = K$$

   Find a general expression for the potential at a distance r cm if $V = 40$ at $r = 5$ and $V = 0$ at $r = 3$.

5E. A rocket, of mass m kg, is projected vertically upwards with a speed of u ms^{-1} from a point on the Earth's surface. When it is at a distance, s metres, from the centre of the Earth, it is subject to a gravitational force of magnitude $\frac{mgr^2}{s^2}$ newtons directed towards the centre of the Earth, where r metres is the radius of the Earth. If its velocity is v ms^{-1} vertically upwards when its distance from the centre of the Earth is s metres, then its equation of motion is given by

   $$v\frac{dv}{ds} = -\frac{gr^2}{s^2}.$$

   (a) Show that $v^2 = u^2 - 2gr(1 - \frac{r}{s})$.

   (b) Taking $g = 9.8$ and $r = 6.4 \times 10^6$, find the value of s when $v = 0$ if $u = 5600$.

   (c) What does this value of s represent?

   (d) What can you say about the value of u if the rocket never stops moving away from Earth?

3.2　Particular integrals

A vat used in a brewing process is cleaned by a scrubbing device which can move up and down inside the vat. Jets supply clean water for the scrubbing process and to flush out the tank.

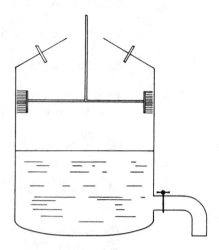

The scrubbing device needs to stay above the level of the liquid. The designer therefore needs to know how the depth of the liquid will vary with time.

The designer has data on how the depth varies with time when the vat drains from an initial depth of 500 cm.

t seconds	0	5	10	15	20	25	30
y cm	500	474	450	428	406	385	367

On the assumption that the rate at which the liquid drains out of the vat is proportional to the depth, the designer proposes the model:

$$\frac{dy}{dt} = -0.01y$$

It is also known that the water jets deliver a total of 20 litres per second and the dimensions of the vat are such that this would increase the depth at 0.5 cms⁻¹.

(a)　**For the depth of liquid during the scrubbing out process, justify the model**

$$\frac{dy}{dt} + 0.01y = 0.5$$

Obtain a symbolic solution.

(b)　**What constant value of y is a solution of the differential equation?**

(c)　**Obtain a symbolic solution for the situation when the water jets are switched off.**

(d)　**How do the solutions in (b) and (c) relate to that for (a)?**

For the differential equations connected with the vat scrubbing problem, it was possible to separate the variables and hence calculate the explicit equation for the solutions.

$$\frac{dy}{dt} + 0.01y = 0$$

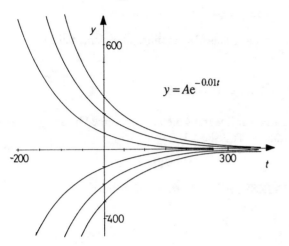

$$y = Ae^{-0.01t}$$

$$\frac{dy}{dt} + 0.01y = 0.5$$

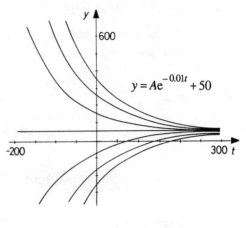

$$y = Ae^{-0.01t} + 50$$

In practice, it takes time to open and close the control valves and so the rates of flow are likely to be time dependent. For such cases, a solution can be sketched even if the method of separating the variables cannot be used.

$$\frac{dy}{dt} + 0.01y = 0.025t$$

$$\frac{dy}{dt} + 0.01y = 0.5 - 0.025t$$

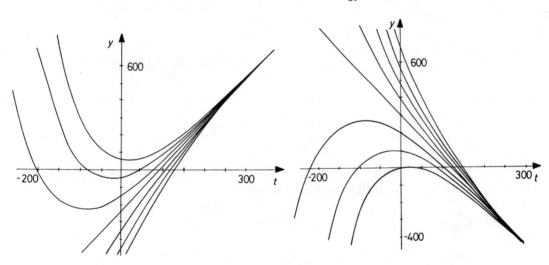

The general solution of

$$\frac{dy}{dt} + 0.01y = 0.5$$

can be thought of as the sum of $Ae^{-0.01t}$ with the particular integral, $y = 50$.

The particular integral was obvious from the graph. The families of exponential solution curves for each of

$$\frac{dy}{dt} + 0.01y = 0.025t \qquad \frac{dy}{dt} + 0.01y = 0.5 - 0.025t$$

also appear to be arranged around a particular integral which is represented by a straight line. This is investigated further on Tasksheet 1.

 TASKSHEET 1 – *Particular integrals*

Example 3

Find a particular integral for $\frac{dy}{dt} + 0.01y = 1.25 \sin 0.02t$.

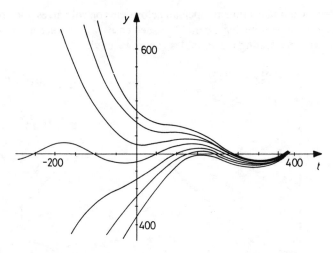

[As shown in the sketch, the family of solution curves appear to be twisted about a solution which is represented by a sine wave.]

Solution

Let $y = A \sin 0.02t + B \cos 0.02t$, then

$$0.02 (A \cos 0.02t - B \sin 0.02t) + 0.01 (A \sin 0.02t + B \cos 0.02t) = 1.25 \sin 0.02t$$

$$\Rightarrow \quad 0.02A + 0.01B = 0,$$
$$-0.02B + 0.01A = 1.25$$

$$\Rightarrow A = 25, B = -50$$

A particular integral is $25 \sin 0.02t - 50 \cos 0.02t$.

Exercise 2

1. Find a particular integral for each of the following differential equations.

    (a) $\frac{dx}{dt} + 2x = 6$ Try $x = A$

    (b) $\frac{dx}{dt} + 2x = 4t.$ Try $x = A + Bt$

    (c) $\frac{dx}{dt} + 2x = 4t + 6$ Try $x = A + Bt$

    (d) $\frac{dx}{dt} + 2x = t^2$ Try $x = A + Bt + Ct^2$

    (e) $\frac{dx}{dt} + 2x = t^2 + 4t$ Try $x = A + Bt + Ct^2$

    (f) $\frac{dx}{dt} + 2x = t^2 + 4t - 6$ Try $x = A + Bt + Ct^2$

2. Comment on any features you may have noticed in the answers to question 1. Use the results of question 1 to write down a particular integral to the differential equation $\frac{dx}{dt} + 2x = t^2 - 4t + 6.$

3. Find particular integrals for the following differential equations.

    (a) $\frac{dy}{dx} + 0.4y = 1.2$ (b) $\frac{dv}{dr} + 0.4v = 2.4r$

    (c) $\frac{dp}{dy} + 0.4p = 6.4y^2$ (d) $\frac{dh}{dt} + 0.4h = 1.2 + 2.4t + 6.4t^2$

4. Find a particular integral for each of the following differential equations.

    (a) $\frac{dy}{dt} - 2.5y = 7.3e^{2t}$ Try $y = Ae^{2t}$

    (b) $\frac{dr}{dx} + 0.8r = 3.2e^{-4x}$ Try $r = Ae^{-4x}$

    (c) $\frac{dV}{ds} + 2V = 1.6 \sin 4s$ Try $V = A \sin 4s + B \cos 4s$

    (d) $\frac{df}{dz} - 1.5f = 7.5 \cos 3z$ Try $f = A \sin 3z + B \cos 3z$

5. Find a particular integral for each of the following differential equations

    (a) $\frac{dy}{dt} - 2y = e^{5t}$

    (b) $\frac{dy}{dt} - 2y = \sin 4t$

    (c) $\frac{dy}{dt} - 2y = 3 \sin 4t + 6e^{5t}$

3.3 Linear equations

The general solution to the differential equation $\frac{dx}{dt} + 0.01x = 0.5 - 0.0025t$ can be obtained as the sum of two parts.

(1) A solution of the equation, for example $-0.25t + 75$. This is referred to as the particular integral (PI).

(2) The general solution to $\frac{dx}{dt} + 0.01x = 0$, which is $Ae^{-0.01t}$. This is known as the complementary function (CF).

You have also seen that PI's have an additive property; a PI for $\frac{dx}{dt} + 0.1x = 0.5$ added to a PI for $\frac{dx}{dt} + 0.1x = -0.0025t$ is a PI for $\frac{dx}{dt} + 0.1x = 0.5 - 0.0025t$.

This additive property of solutions is characteristic of the class of differential equations known as linear differential equations. In general, a first order linear differential equation has the form $\frac{dy}{dx} + p(x)y = q(x)$ where $p(x)$ and $q(x)$ are both functions of x. The equation is linear in the sense that $\frac{dy}{dx}$ and y are not raised to any powers.

 TASKSHEET 2 – *Linearity*

> The general solution of a differential equation of the form
>
> $$\frac{dy}{dx} + p(x)y = q(x)$$
>
> can be expressed as
>
> complementary function (CF) + particular integral (PI).

Example 4

Solve $\frac{dy}{dx} - y = 4e^{3x}$, given that $y = 0$ when $x = 0$.

Solution

For a PI, try $y = Ke^{3x}$.

$$3Ke^{3x} - Ke^{3x} = 4e^{3x} \Rightarrow K = 2$$

The CF is $y = Ae^x$.

The general solution is $y = Ae^x + 2e^{3x}$, where $0 = A + 2$.

Then $A = -2$ and the particular solution is $y = 2e^{3x} - 2e^x$.

Exercise 3

1. For each of the following differential equations, find the CF and a PI. Hence find the general solution and a solution which passes through the origin.

   (a) $\dfrac{dy}{dx} + 3y = 24$ 　　　　(b) $\dfrac{dy}{dx} + 2y = 2x$

   (c) $\dfrac{dy}{dx} + 2y = -7$ 　　　　(d) $\dfrac{dy}{dx} + 2y = 2x - 7$

2. Find the general solution of each of the following differential equations.

   (a) $\dfrac{dy}{dx} - 2y = 12$ 　　　　(b) $\dfrac{dy}{dt} + 8y = 10$

   (c) $\dfrac{dP}{dt} + 3P = 0$ 　　　　(d) $\dfrac{dV}{dh} - V = 5 - 5h$

   (e) $\dfrac{dy}{dx} + 2y = e^x$

3E. (a) Try $y = Ke^{4x}$ as a particular integral for $\dfrac{dy}{dx} - 4y = 3e^{4x}$.

   Explain why this is not possible.

   (b) Try $y = Kxe^{4x}$ instead. Write down the general solution.

   (c) Find the general solution of:

   (i) $\dfrac{dy}{dx} + 2y = e^{-2x}$

   (ii) $\dfrac{dy}{dx} - 6y = 3e^{6x}$

 TASKSHEET 3E - *Integrating factors*

After working through this chapter you should:

1. know how to solve differential equations by the method of separating variables:

$$\frac{dy}{dx} = \frac{f(x)}{g(y)} \implies \int g(y)\, dy = \int f(x)\, dx$$

2. be able to find particular integrals for simple cases of linear, first order, differential equations;

3. understand how to solve linear differential equations by adding the complementary function to a particular integral;

4. know that the general solution of

$$\frac{dy}{dx} + ky = 0, \text{ where } k \text{ is constant,}$$

is given by

$$y = Ae^{-kx}$$

Particular integrals

1. A particular integral for $\frac{dy}{dt} + 0.01y = 0.5$ was represented on the sketch by a horizontal straight line. $y = C$ satisfies the equation providing $0.01C = 0.5$ and so the particular integral was $y = 50$.

    Similarly, find C if $y = C$ is a solution to the differential equation $\frac{dy}{dt} - 2.5y = 7.4$.

2. $\frac{dy}{dt} + 0.01y = 0.025t$ appears to have a solution represented on the sketch by a straight line. $y = A + Bt$ satisfies the equation providing $B + 0.01(A + Bt) = 0.025t$.

    Explain why $B = 2.5$ and find the necessary value for A.

3. Find A and B if $y = A + Bt$ is to be a particular integral for $\frac{dy}{dt} + 0.01y = 0.5 - 0.025t$.

4. Two families of solution curves are sketched below.

    $$\frac{dy}{dt} + 0.01y = 0.0001t^2 + 0.03t - 1 \qquad\qquad \frac{dy}{dt} + 0.01y = 0.3e^{0.02t}$$

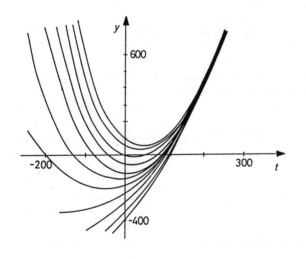
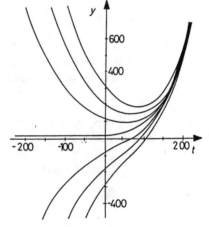

    In the first case, the solution curves appear to be arranged around a quadratic particular integral; in the second case they are arranged around an exponential curve.

    Find particular integrals for

    (a) $\frac{dy}{dt} + 0.01y = 0.0001t^2 + 0.03t - 1$

    (b) $\frac{dy}{dt} + 0.01y = 0.3e^{0.02t}$

Linearity

1. Find $\frac{dy}{dx} - 3y$ for:

   (a) $y = \sin x$ (b) $y = \frac{1}{x}$ (c) $y = \sin x + \frac{1}{x}$

2. Find $\frac{dy}{dx} + 5y$ for:

   (a) $y = 4$ (b) $y = x$ (c) $y = 4 + x$

3. Find $\frac{dy}{dx} + x^2 y$ for:

   (a) $y = x^2$ (b) $y = 5x$

   (c) $y = e^x$ (d) $y = x^2 + 5x + e^x$

4. Find $\frac{dy}{dx} + y^2$ for:

   (a) $y = 4$ (b) $y = x$ (c) $y = 4 + x$

5. $\frac{dy}{dx} + y^2$ is **not** linear in $\frac{dy}{dx}$ and y. Describe how the answers to questions 1 to 4 illustrate the difference between linear and non-linear expressions.

6E. Find $\frac{dy}{dx} + p(x)y$ for $y = y_1 + y_2$. Use your answer to explain why the general solution for the differential equation

   $$\frac{dy}{dx} + p(x)y = q(x)$$

   is of the form

        complementary function + particular integral.

Integrating factors

A differential equation of the form

$$\frac{d}{dx}(e^{5x}y) = 2e^{5x} \qquad ①$$

can be solved easily:

$$e^{5x}y = 2\int e^{5x}\,dx$$
$$\Rightarrow e^{5x}y = \frac{2}{5}e^{5x} + c$$
$$\Rightarrow \quad y = \frac{2}{5} + ce^{-5x}$$

However, the original differential equation is the same as

$$e^{5x}\frac{dy}{dx} + 5e^{5x}y = 2e^{5x}$$

i.e. $\quad \dfrac{dy}{dx} + 5y = 2 \qquad ②$

This is precisely the type of equation considered in this chapter. An alternative method of solving an equation such as ② is to multiply by a factor, called an **integrating factor**, to convert the equation into a form which can be solved as above.

For the equation $\dfrac{dy}{dx} + 5y = 2$, the integrating factor is e^{5x}. This would convert equation ② into equation ①.

1. Solve each of the following equations, using the given integrating factor (IF).

    (a) $\quad \dfrac{dy}{dx} + 3y = 7 \qquad \text{IF} = e^{3x}$

    (b) $\quad \dfrac{dy}{dx} - 2y = 9 \qquad \text{IF} = e^{-2x}$

    (c) $\quad \dfrac{dy}{dx} + y = x \qquad \text{IF} = e^{x}$

2. (a) For k constant, what would be the integrating factor for an equation of the form

    $$\frac{dy}{dx} + ky = q(x)\,?$$

    (b) What is a possible disadvantage of the method of integrating factors?

The method of integrating factors has the considerable advantage that it can be used for first order linear equations in cases where the coefficients are **not** constant and where particular integrals may be very difficult to spot. In addition, it has the advantage of being a systematic method, simply requiring the carrying out of specific integrations.

(continued)

In general, the integrating factor is found as follows:

> **For an equation of the form**
>
> $$\frac{dy}{dx} + p(x)y = q(x)$$
>
> **the integrating factor is** $e^{\int p(x)\,dx}$.

Example

Solve $\dfrac{dy}{dx} + \dfrac{1}{x}y = x^2$

Solution

$\displaystyle\int \frac{1}{x}\,dx = \ln x$ and so the integrating factor is $e^{\ln x} = x$. [Note that the constant of integration can be ignored.]

Then
$$x\frac{dy}{dx} + y = x^3$$

$$\Rightarrow \quad \frac{d}{dx}(xy) = x^3$$

$$\Rightarrow \quad xy = \frac{1}{4}x^4 + c$$

$$\Rightarrow \quad y = \frac{1}{4}x^3 + \frac{c}{x}$$

3.   Use the method of integrating factors to find the general solution for

$$\frac{dy}{dx} + \frac{3}{x}y = \frac{1}{x}.$$

4.   Solve the following equations

(a) $\dfrac{dy}{dx} + y = e^{-x}, \qquad y = 1$ at $x = 0$

(b) $\dfrac{dy}{dx} + 2xy = 2x, \qquad y = 3$ at $x = 0$

(c) $\dfrac{dy}{dx} - (\tan x)y = 1, \quad y = 0$ at $x = \dfrac{\pi}{4}$

1. Bacteria in a tank of water are increasing at a rate proportional to the number present. Water is draining out of the tank at a rate of 2 litres per hour. Initially the tank contains 100 litres of water.

   (a) Explain why the differential equation

   $$\frac{dN}{dt} = kN - \frac{2N}{100 - 2t}, \quad k \text{ constant}$$

   models the number of bacteria N in the tank at time t hours.

   (b) Solve the differential equation to obtain a symbolic solution for N in terms of N_0, the initial size of the bacteria colony.

   (c) Describe how the number of bacteria in the tank changes as the tank drains.

2. For each of the following families of solution curves, find the differential equations that they represent.

   (a) $y = \dfrac{A}{x^2}$ (b) $y^2 = x + c$ (c) $4(v + 1) = (\ln t + c)^2$

3. Find particular integrals for

   (a) $\dfrac{dy}{dx} + 4y = 5 + 6x$ (b) $\dfrac{dx}{dt} + 3x = 7e^t$ (c) $\dfrac{dy}{dx} - 4y = 3 + x^2$

4. Find the general solutions of the differential equations:

   (a) $\dfrac{dq}{dt} + q = 2 \cos t$ (b) $\dfrac{dq}{dt} + q = 2 \sin t$ (c) $\dfrac{dq}{dt} + q = \cos t + \sin t$

5E. Two plates of a condenser of constant capacity C are connected by a wire of constant resistance R. The differential equation connecting the charge, q, with the electromotive force, E, is

   $$R \frac{dq}{dt} + \frac{q}{C} = E.$$

   Find its solution when

   (a) $E = 0$ (b) $E = E_0$ (constant)   (c) $E = E_0 \cos pt$ (p constant)

   In each case, describe what happens to the charge as $t \to + \infty$.

4 *Second order equations*

4.1 Arbitrary constants

You have seen how second order differential equations can be solved numerically. In this chapter, you will consider their solution by symbolic methods. A simple example of a second order differential equation is provided by the acceleration of a body falling freely under gravity.

The equation which represents the fact that the acceleration is constant (providing the air resistance is negligible) is

$$\frac{d^2y}{dt^2} = -g$$

The value of the acceleration due to gravity is approximately 10 ms⁻².

(a) **Obtain the general solution of** $\dfrac{d^2y}{dt^2} = -10.$

(b) **How many arbitrary constants does your solution possess? In general, explain how and why the number of arbitrary constants is related to the order of a differential equation.**

(c) **For the differential equation** $\dfrac{d^2y}{dt^2} = -10$, **describe possible initial conditions that would determine the values of the arbitrary constants and thus give rise to a particular solution. How many initial conditions would be needed to determine the arbitrary constants for a differential equation of order n?**

In general, a particular solution of a differential equation is obtained by

- finding a general solution;

- using initial conditions to determine the values of the arbitrary constants.

> **The general solution of a differential equation of order n has n arbitrary constants.**
>
> **If the solution also satisfies n initial conditions (or *boundary conditions*), then the values of the constants can be determined, giving rise to a particular solution.**

Example 1

Solve the differential equation $\dfrac{d^2y}{dx^2} = 3$, given that $y = 2$ when $x = 0$ and $y = 6$ when $x = 1$.

Solution

The general solution is obtained by integrating twice.

$$\frac{dy}{dx} = 3x + A$$

$$y = \frac{3}{2}x^2 + Ax + B.$$

Since the given conditions must be satisfied,

$$y = 2 \text{ when } x = 0 \Rightarrow 2 = B$$
$$y = 6 \text{ when } x = 1 \Rightarrow 6 = \frac{3}{2} + A + B$$
$$\Rightarrow A = \frac{5}{2}$$

The particular solution is $y = \dfrac{3}{2}x^2 + \dfrac{5}{2}x + 2.$

For other second order differential equations it is not always immediately clear how to obtain a symbolic solution by two stages of integration. Some methods for obtaining symbolic solutions are given in this chapter. Whichever method is used, a general solution to a second order differential equation always requires two arbitrary constants.

4.2 Linearity

An equation such as

$$\frac{d^2y}{dx^2} - 5\frac{dy}{dx} + 6y = 1$$

is a second order linear equation. The equation is called linear because y and its derivatives, $\frac{dy}{dx}$ and $\frac{d^2y}{dx^2}$, occur only to the first power. (This is similar to the way that x and y occur only to the first power in an equation of a straight line, $ax + by + c = 0$). Some properties of linearity are investigated on Tasksheet 1.

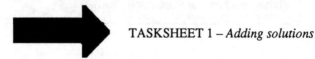

TASKSHEET 1 – *Adding solutions*

Tasksheet 1 suggests that the method of complementary functions and particular integrals extends to second order linear differential equations. The only second order equations which will be considered in this chapter are linear ones with constant coefficients.

> **The general solution of the equation**
>
> $$a\frac{d^2y}{dx^2} + b\frac{dy}{dx} + cy = f(x)$$
>
> **is the sum of a particular integral and the complementary function (with two arbitrary constants).**

Example 2

(a) Find $\frac{d^2y}{dx^2} - 5\frac{dy}{dx} + 6y$ for $y = e^{2x}$ and $y = e^{3x}$.

(b) Hence solve the equation

$$\frac{d^2y}{dx^2} - 5\frac{dy}{dx} + 6y = 12.$$

Solution

(a) For $y = e^{2x}$, $\frac{d^2y}{dx^2} - 5\frac{dy}{dx} + 6y = (4 - 10 + 6)\,e^{2x} = 0$

  For $y = e^{3x}$, $\frac{d^2y}{dx^2} - 5\frac{dy}{dx} + 6y = (9 - 15 + 6)\,e^{3x} = 0$

(b) An obvious particular solution is $y = 2$.

  The general solution is $Ae^{2x} + Be^{3x} + 2$.

4.3 The auxiliary equation

You have seen that a first order linear equation with constant coefficients has an exponential complementary function. For example, $\frac{dy}{dx} + 2y = 0$ has solution $y = Ae^{-2x}$.

For a second order equation with constant coefficients, a complementary function will have two arbitrary constants. The precise form of the complementary function is studied on Tasksheet 2.

 TASKSHEET 2 – *Complementary functions*

> For the differential equation
>
> $$a\,\frac{d^2y}{dx^2} + b\,\frac{dy}{dx} + cy = f(x)$$
>
> the equation $am^2 + bm + c = 0$ is called the *auxiliary equation*.
>
> If the roots of the auxiliary equation are α and β, then the complementary function is $y = Ae^{\alpha x} + Be^{\beta x}$.

> **Under what circumstances would the auxiliary equation method *not* produce a complementary function with two arbitrary constants?**

Example 3

Find the general solution of

$$\frac{d^2x}{dt^2} - 3\frac{dx}{dt} - 4x = 4$$

Solution

The auxiliary equation is $m^2 - 3m - 4 = 0$

$$\Leftrightarrow (m + 1)(m - 4) = 0$$
$$\Leftrightarrow \qquad\qquad m = -1 \text{ or } 4$$

The complementary function is $x = Ae^{-t} + Be^{4t}$.

-1 is a particular integral and so the general solution is

$$x = Ae^{-t} + Be^{4t} - 1$$

4.4 General solutions

The general strategy for solving a second order linear equation with constant coefficients of the form

$$a \frac{d^2y}{dx^2} + b \frac{dy}{dx} + cy = f(x)$$

is as follows:

- solve the auxiliary equation to obtain the complementary function;

- find a particular integral;

- form the general solution by adding the CF and PI;

- if a particular solution is required, use two boundary conditions to determine the values of the two arbitrary constants.

To find a particular integral it is usual to assume that it has the same form as $f(x)$ and then use the differential equation to determine suitable values for any constants.

 TASKSHEET 3 – *Particular integrals*

Example 4

Find the general solution of

$$\frac{d^2x}{dt^2} - 3 \frac{dx}{dt} - 4x = 4t - 9$$

Solution

Let $x = at + b$, then

$$-3a - 4(at + b) = 4t - 9$$
$$\Rightarrow a = -1, \quad b = 3.$$

The auxiliary equation is $m^2 - 3m - 4 = 0$
$$\Leftrightarrow (m + 1)(m - 4) = 0$$

The general solution is

$$x = Ae^{-t} + Be^{4t} + 3 - t$$

Exercise 1

1. Find the general solution of

$$\frac{d^2y}{dx^2} - 5\frac{dy}{dx} + 6y = e^x$$

2. Find the solution of

$$\frac{d^2x}{dt^2} - 3\frac{dx}{dt} + 2x = 4t$$

for which $\frac{dx}{dt} = 3$ and $x = 5$ when $t = 0$.

3. Solve $\frac{d^2x}{dt^2} = 4t$, given that $x = 5$ and $\frac{dx}{dt} = 3$ when $t = 0$.

4. Write down the auxiliary equation for the differential equation

$$\frac{d^2y}{dx^2} + 3\frac{dy}{dx} - 10y = 0$$

and hence find the general solution.

5. (a) Write down the auxiliary equation for the differential equation

$$\frac{d^2y}{dx^2} - 4\frac{dy}{dx} + 3y = 6x - 8$$

and hence find the complementary function.

(b) Find a particular integral in the form $y = ax + b$ and thus the general solution to the differential equation.

6. Solve the differential equation $\frac{d^2y}{dx^2} = 4y$, given that $y = 2$ and $\frac{dy}{dx} = 2$ when $x = 0$.

7. Solve $\frac{d^2y}{dx^2} + 4\frac{dy}{dx} + 3y = 4e^x$

43

4.5 Substitution

Most differential equations have to be solved numerically. However, you have developed methods for solving symbolically certain types of differential equations:

- first order equations with separable variables;

- first order linear equations;

- second order linear equations with constant coefficients.

Sometimes other differential equations can be transformed into one of these equations by means of a suitable substitution. Considerable experience is needed to know precisely which substitutions work in various circumstances. In the following examples and exercise the substitution will always be specified.

In the next example, a second order equation with non-constant coefficients is transformed into one with constant coefficients.

Example 5

By using the substitution $y = \frac{z}{x}$, find the general solution of the equation

$$x\frac{d^2y}{dx^2} + (3x+2)\frac{dy}{dx} + (2x+3)y = 0$$

Solution

$$y = \frac{z}{x} \Rightarrow \frac{dy}{dx} = \frac{1}{x}\frac{dz}{dx} - \frac{1}{x^2}z$$

$$\Rightarrow \frac{d^2y}{dx^2} = \frac{1}{x}\frac{d^2z}{dx^2} - \frac{2}{x^2}\frac{dz}{dx} + \frac{2}{x^3}z$$

Substituting for y, $\frac{dy}{dx}$ and $\frac{d^2y}{dx^2}$ in the differential equation,

$$x\left(\frac{1}{x}\frac{d^2z}{dx^2} - \frac{2}{x^2}\frac{dz}{dx} + \frac{2}{x^3}z\right) + (3x+2)\left(\frac{1}{x}\frac{dz}{dx} - \frac{1}{x^2}z\right) + (2x+3)\frac{z}{x} = 0$$

$$\Leftrightarrow \frac{d^2z}{dx^2} + 3\frac{dz}{dx} + 2z = 0$$

$$\Leftrightarrow z = Ae^{-x} + Be^{-2x}$$

$$\Leftrightarrow y = \frac{1}{x}\left(Ae^{-x} + Be^{-2x}\right)$$

> **To transform a differential equation:**
>
> - **find all derivatives in terms of the new variables;**
>
> - **substitute for these derivatives in the original equation.**

For linear equations with constant coefficients, you already know the method of using complementary functions and particular integrals. However, transformations can be used to show how this method is equivalent to repeated integration and therefore why a second order equation has a complementary function with two arbitrary constants. Furthermore, transformations will be used in the next section to demonstrate how to deal with the awkward case of an auxiliary equation with equal roots. Example 6 is a simple case of a substitution reducing a second order equation to two first order equations which have to be solved successively.

Example 6

Use the transformation $z = \frac{dy}{dx} + 2y$ to help solve the equation

$$\frac{d^2y}{dx^2} + 3\frac{dy}{dx} + 2y = 0$$

Solution

$$z = \frac{dy}{dx} + 2y \implies \frac{dz}{dx} = \frac{d^2y}{dx^2} + 2\frac{dy}{dx}$$

Substituting in the differential equation gives

$$\frac{dz}{dx} + z = 0$$

$$\implies z = Ae^{-x}$$

Then $\frac{dy}{dx} + 2y = Ae^{-x}$

$$\implies y = Ae^{-x} + Be^{-2x}$$

Exercise 2

1. Use the substitution $z = \frac{dy}{dx} - 3y$ to help solve the equation

$$\frac{d^2y}{dx^2} - 2\frac{dy}{dx} - 3y = 3x - 1$$

2. By using the substitution $z = \frac{dy}{dx} - y$, solve the equation

$$\frac{d^2y}{dx^2} - y = 2\sin x$$

given that $y = 1$ and $\frac{dy}{dx} = 0$ when $x = 0$.

3E. Solve the differential quation

$$\frac{dy}{dx} = \frac{y}{x} + x^2$$

by using the substitution $y = xz$.

4E. Use the substitution $y = z^2$ to help solve the non-linear equation

$$\frac{dy}{dx} + 2y = 4\sqrt{y}$$

given that $y = 0$ when $x = 0$.

45

4.6   Equal roots

The auxiliary equation for

$$\frac{d^2y}{dx^2} + 4\frac{dy}{dx} + 4y = 0$$

has equal roots and gives rise to a complementary function, Ae^{-2x}, with only one arbitrary constant.

> **Carry out the auxiliary equation method for**
> $$\frac{d^2y}{dx^2} + 4\frac{dy}{dx} + 4y = 0$$
> **and justify the statement above.**

The method of substitution introduced in the previous section can be used to show how to proceed in such cases.

Example 7

Use the substitution $z = e^{2x}y$ to find the general solution of

$$\frac{d^2y}{dx^2} + 4\frac{dy}{dx} + 4y = 0$$

Solution

$$z = e^{2x}y$$

$$\Rightarrow \frac{dz}{dx} = e^{2x}\left(\frac{dy}{dx} + 2y\right)$$

$$\Rightarrow \frac{d^2z}{dx^2} = e^{2x}\left(\frac{d^2y}{dx^2} + 4\frac{dy}{dx} + 4\right)$$

The differential equation therefore becomes

$$\frac{d^2z}{dx^2} = 0$$

$$\Rightarrow \quad z = Ax + B$$

$$\Rightarrow ye^{2x} = Ax + B$$

$$\Rightarrow \quad y = (Ax + B)e^{-2x}$$

In the example above, the auxiliary equation had -2 as a repeated root and the complementary function was

$$(Ax + B)e^{-2x}$$

The same idea works for **any** auxiliary equation with repeated roots. In practice, there is therefore no need to repeat the process of Example 7. Instead, you can just quote the following result.

> **If a quadratic auxiliary equation has a repeated root α, then the complementary function is**
> $$(Ax + B)e^{\alpha x}$$

Example 8

Solve the equation $\dfrac{d^2y}{dx^2} + 2\dfrac{dy}{dx} + y = x$ given that $\dfrac{dy}{dx} = y = 0$ when $x = 0$.

Solution

A particular integral is $x - 2$.

The auxiliary equation, $m^2 + 2m + 1 = 0$, has repeated root -1.

The general solution is therefore $y = (Ax + B)e^{-x} + x - 2$.

$$y = (Ax + B)e^{-x} + x - 2$$
$$\frac{dy}{dx} = (A - Ax - B)e^{-x} + 1$$

When $x = 0$, $0 = B - 2$ and $0 = A - B + 1$

$$\Rightarrow A = 1 \text{ and } B = 2$$

The particular solution is $y = (x + 2)e^{-x} + x - 2$.

Exercise 3

1. Solve $\dfrac{d^2y}{dx^2} - 2\dfrac{dy}{dx} + y = 7$

2. Solve $\dfrac{d^2y}{dx^2} + 6\dfrac{dy}{dx} + 9y = x$

3. Solve $16\dfrac{d^2y}{dx^2} + 8\dfrac{dy}{dx} + y = 0$

4. Solve $\dfrac{d^2y}{dx^2} - 10\dfrac{dy}{dx} + 25y = 9e^{2x}$, given that $y = \dfrac{dy}{dx} = 0$ when $x = 0$

5. For a particular integral to

    $$\frac{d^2y}{dx^2} - 7\frac{dy}{dx} + 10y = e^{2x}$$

    try both Ae^{2x} and Axe^{2x}. Comment on your answers.

4.7   Complex roots

The differential equation

$$\frac{d^2y}{dx^2} + y = 0$$

has auxiliary equation $m^2 + 1 = 0$. This has complex roots $\pm j$ and so the methods used so far in this chapter would indicate that the general solution is $Ae^{jx} + Be^{-jx}$.

However, this differential equation models various important physical situations and therefore must have a real solution. Consider, for example, a particle moving around a circle of radius 1 unit, with angular speed of 1 rad s^{-1}.

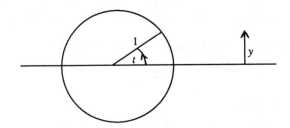

The height of the particle above the reference line is given by $y = \cos t$.

Then $\dfrac{dy}{dt} = -\sin t$ and $\dfrac{d^2y}{dt^2} = -\cos t$.

The height therefore satisfies the differential equation

$$\frac{d^2y}{dt^2} + y = 0$$

A method for obtaining real solutions for second order linear differential equations whose auxiliary equations have complex roots is developed in the next tasksheet.

TASKSHEET 4 – *Complex roots*

> **If the roots of the auxiliary equation are**
>
> $$\upsilon \pm \omega j$$
>
> **then the complementary function is of the form**
>
> $$e^{\upsilon x} (A \cos \omega x + B \sin \omega x)$$

Example 9

Solve $\frac{d^2y}{dx^2} - 2\frac{dy}{dx} + 5 = 0$, given that $y = 2$ when $x = 0$ and $y = 4e^{\frac{\pi}{4}}$ when $x = \frac{\pi}{4}$.

Solution

The auxiliary equation is $m^2 - 2m + 5 = 0$

$$\Leftrightarrow m = \frac{2 \pm \sqrt{(4-20)}}{2}$$

$$\Leftrightarrow m = 1 \pm 2j$$

$CF = e^x (A \cos 2x + B \sin 2x)$

When $x = 0, \quad 2 = A$

When $x = \frac{\pi}{4}, \quad 4e^{\frac{\pi}{4}} = Be^{\frac{\pi}{4}} \Rightarrow B = 4$

$y = e^x (2 \cos 2x + 4 \sin 2x)$

Exercise 4

1. Find the general solution of

    (a) $\frac{d^2y}{dx^2} - 2\frac{dy}{dx} + 2y = 0$

    (b) $\frac{d^2y}{dx^2} - 2\frac{dy}{dx} + 2y = x$

2. Solve the differential equation

    $$\frac{d^2x}{dt^2} + x = t$$

    given that $x = 0$ and $\frac{dx}{dt} = 2$ when $t = 0$.

3E. The current I amps in an electrical circuit at time t seconds satisfies the differential equation

    $$\frac{d^2I}{dt^2} + 2\frac{dI}{dt} + 10I = 2 \cos t + 9 \sin t$$

    Initially, $I = 0$ and $\frac{dI}{dt} = 0$. Find the current at time t seconds.

After working through this chapter you should:

1. know that the number of arbitrary constants in the general solution to a differential equation is equal to the order of the equation;

2. be able to use boundary conditions to determine the value of arbitrary constants;

3. understand how to find particular integrals in simple cases;

4. be able to find complementary functions for all second order linear differential equations with constant coefficients, including those for which the auxiliary equation has equal roots or complex roots;

5. know how to obtain the general solution to a second order linear differential equation by adding a particular integral and the complementary function;

6. be able to transform a differential equation using a given substitution.

Adding solutions

1. (a) By substitution, show that $y = e^{-3x}$ is a solution of the differential equation

$$\frac{d^2y}{dx^2} + \frac{dy}{dx} - 6y = 0$$

(b) Show that $y = Ae^{-3x}$, where A is an arbitrary constant, is also a solution.

(c) Show that $y = Be^{2x}$ is another solution.

(d) Check whether $y = Ae^{-3x} + Be^{2x}$ is also a solution.

2. (a) Show that $y = x^2$ is a particular integral for

$$\frac{d^2y}{dx^2} + \frac{dy}{dx} - 6y = 2 + 2x - 6x^2$$

(b) Check that $y = Ae^{-3x} + Be^{2x} + x^2$ also satisfies the differential equation.

3. (a) Show that $y = Ae^{-x} + Be^{-2x}$ is a solution of the differential equation

$$\frac{d^2y}{dx^2} + 3\frac{dy}{dx} + 2y = 0$$

(b) Show that $y = e^x$ is a particular solution of the differential equation

$$\frac{d^2y}{dx^2} + 3\frac{dy}{dx} + 2y = 6e^x$$

(c) Explain why you might expect $y = Ae^{-x} + Be^{-2x} + e^x$ to be the general solution.

4. $y = \sin 2x$ is a particular solution for the differential equation

$$\frac{d^2y}{dx^2} + 3\frac{dy}{dx} + 2y = 6\cos 2x - 2\sin 2x$$

Suggest a possible general solution for this equation and check your answer.

5. Find $\dfrac{d^2y}{dx^2} - 7\dfrac{dy}{dx} + 10y$ for each of the following.

(a) $y = x^2$ (b) $y = e^x$ (c) $y = x^2 + e^x$

(d) $y = e^{2x}$ (e) $y = Ae^{2x} + x^2$

6E. (a) If y_1 and y_2 each satisfy the equation $\dfrac{d^2y}{dx^2} - 5\dfrac{dy}{dx} + 6y = 0$, then show that $y = y_1 + y_2$ also satisfies the equation.

(b) If the equation $\dfrac{d^2y}{dx^2} - 5\dfrac{dy}{dx} + 6y = 1$ is satisfied by y_3, then show that it is also satisfied by $Ay_1 + By_2 + y_3$.

Complementary functions

1. For any function of the form $y = e^{mx}$, find $\frac{dy}{dx}$ and $\frac{d^2y}{dx^2}$.

2. Show that $y = e^{mx}$ is a solution of $\frac{d^2y}{dx^2} - 7\frac{dy}{dx} + 10\,y = 0$ providing $m^2 - 7m + 10 = 0$.

   Find the possible values of m. Hence find the general solution of the differential equation.

3. Find the condition for $y = e^{mx}$ to be a solution of $\frac{d^2y}{dx^2} - 5\frac{dy}{dx} + 6y = 0$.

   Solve the equation, given that $y = 1$ and $\frac{dy}{dx} = 2$ when $x = 0$.

4. For each of the following differential equations, write down the condition on m for $y = e^{mx}$ to be a solution.

   (a) $\dfrac{d^2y}{dx^2} + 5\dfrac{dy}{dx} + 4y = 0$

   (b) $\dfrac{d^2y}{dx^2} - \dfrac{dy}{dx} - 12y = 0$

   (c) $\dfrac{d^2y}{dx^2} + 2\dfrac{dy}{dx} + y = 0$

   (d) $\dfrac{d^2y}{dx^2} + y = 0$

   (e) $\dfrac{d^2y}{dx^2} - 8y = 0$

   (f) $a\dfrac{d^2y}{dx^2} + b\dfrac{dy}{dx} + cy = 0$

Particular integrals

1. For the equation $\dfrac{d^2y}{dx^2} - 5\dfrac{dy}{dx} + 6y = x$, suppose that $y = ax + b$ is a particular integral, where a and b are constants whose values are to be determined.

    Find $\dfrac{dy}{dx}$ and $\dfrac{d^2y}{dx^2}$ in terms of a and b and substitute into the differential equation. Hence find the particular integral.

2. Find particular integrals for the following differential equations.

    (a) $\dfrac{d^2y}{dx^2} - 7\dfrac{dy}{dx} + 10y = 3$ [Try $y = k$ and find k]

    (b) $\dfrac{d^2y}{dx^2} - 7\dfrac{dy}{dx} + 10y = 20x - 64$ [Try $y = ax + b$ and find a and b]

    (c) $\dfrac{d^2y}{dx^2} - 7\dfrac{dy}{dx} + 10y = 10x^2 - 14x + 22$ [Try $y = ax^2 + bx + c$ and find a, b and c]

    (d) $\dfrac{d^2y}{dx^2} - 7\dfrac{dy}{dx} + 10y = 8e^x$ [Try $y = Ce^x$ and find C]

    (e) $\dfrac{d^2y}{dx^2} - 7\dfrac{dy}{dx} + 10y = e^{3x}$ [Try $y = Ce^{3x}$ and find C]

    (f) $\dfrac{d^2y}{dx^2} - 7\dfrac{dy}{dx} + 10y = \sin x$ [Try $y = a \sin x + b \cos x$ and find a and b]

3. For the equation $\dfrac{d^2y}{dx^2} + 4y = 3 \sin x + 6 \cos x$, find a particular integral in the form of

    $y = a \sin x + b \cos x$.

Complex roots

1. (a) Find the second derivative of each of $\cos x$ and $\sin x$.

    (b) What differential equation is satisfied by both $y = \cos x$ and $y = \sin x$?

    (c) Show that $y = A \cos x + B \sin x$ is a general solution of $\dfrac{d^2y}{dx^2} + y = 0$.

Although the differential equation $\dfrac{d^2y}{dx^2} + y = 0$ has an auxiliary equation with complex roots it has

a real general solution of the form $A \sin x + B \cos x$. The connection between the real solution and the auxiliary equation is considered in question 2.

2. (a) For $\dfrac{d^2y}{dx^2} + y = 0$, show that the auxiliary equation method leads to a

    complementary function of the form

    $$Ce^{jx} + De^{-jx}$$

    (b) Use the relationships

    $$e^{jx} = \cos x + j \sin x$$
    $$e^{-jx} = \cos x - j \sin x$$

    to express the complementary function in the form $A \cos x + B \sin x$.

The solution to question 2 demonstrates that the apparently complex solution $Ce^{jx} + De^{-jx}$ is equivalent to the real solution $A \cos x + B \sin x$. In practice, it is better to start immediately from the trigonometric form of the complementary function. The general method is developed in the remaining questions of this tasksheet.

3. (a) Find the second derivative of each of $\cos 3x$ and $\sin 3x$.

    (b) Suggest a possible form for the general solution of $\dfrac{d^2y}{dx^2} + 9y = 0$. Check your

    answer by substitution into the differential equation.

(continued)

54

4.   State general solutions for

   (a) $\dfrac{d^2y}{dx^2} + 16y = 0$

   (b) $\dfrac{d^2s}{dt^2} + 4s = 0$

   (c) $\dfrac{d^2y}{dx^2} + \omega^2 y = 0$

   (d) $\dfrac{d^2u}{dv^2} + 2u = 0$

   (e) $\dfrac{d^2x}{dt^2} + 5x = 0$

5.   Find the solution of $\dfrac{d^2y}{dx^2} + 9y = 0$ such that $y = 0$ and $\dfrac{dy}{dx} = 1$ when $x = 0$.

You have seen that if the auxiliary equation has roots $\pm\, \omega j$, then the complementary function is of the form

   $A \, \cos \omega x + B \sin \omega x$

The general case of an auxiliary equation with roots $\upsilon \pm \omega j$ is dealt with in questions 6 and 7.

6.   (a)   For the differential equation

   $$\dfrac{d^2y}{dx^2} - 2\dfrac{dy}{dx} + 10y = 0$$

   (i)   use the substitution $y = e^x z$ to obtain the complementary function;

   (ii)   find the roots of the auxiliary equation.

   (b)   What do your results suggest for the complementary function if the auxiliary equation has roots $\upsilon \pm \omega j$?

7E.   (a)   For the differential equation

   $$\dfrac{d^2y}{dx^2} - 2\upsilon\dfrac{dy}{dx} + (\upsilon^2 + \omega^2)y = 0$$

   (i)   use the substitution $y = e^{\upsilon x} z$ to obtain the complementary function;

   (ii)   find the roots of the auxiliary equation.

   (b)   Comment on your results in (a).

A differential equation of the form $\dfrac{d^2x}{dt^2} + \omega^2 x = 0$ is said to be a differential equation of simple harmonic motion (SHM). Such an equation occurs in a number of important contexts including:

• the motion of a simple pendulum;

• the vibrations of a tuning fork and various musical instruments;

• the vibrations of an electron generating light waves;

• the growth and decay of a colony of bacteria in interaction with food supply and waste products.

1.	A familiar example of SHM is the motion of an object fixed to the end of an oscillating spring. Suppose such an object satisfies the equation

$$\frac{d^2x}{dt^2} + 4x = 0$$

where x is the object's displacement in metres.

(a)	What is the physical significance of $\dfrac{d^2x}{dt^2}$? Describe the meaning of the equation

$$\frac{d^2x}{dt^2} + 4x = 0 \text{ in your own words.}$$

(b)	Solve the differential equation given that $x = 0.1$ and $\dfrac{dx}{dt} = 0.2$ when $t = 0$.

(c)	Express your solution in the form $C \sin(\omega t + \varepsilon)$. Sketch your solution and describe the significance of C and ω.

2.	If there is an additional frictional resistance force which is assumed to be proportional to the velocity, the acceleration might be given by the equation

$$\frac{d^2x}{dt^2} + 5\frac{dx}{dt} + 4x = 0$$

(a)	Find the general solution of this equation.

(b)	The motion in this case is said to be **heavily damped**. What feature of your solution is highlighted by this terminology?

(continued)

3.   Suppose $\dfrac{d^2x}{dt^2} + 6\dfrac{dx}{dt} + 13x = 0$.

     (a)   Solve this differential equation given that $x = 0$ and $\dfrac{dx}{dt} = 0.2$ when $t = 0$.

     (b)   Sketch your solution and explain why such motion is said to be **lightly damped.**

The solutions of the previous questions have only involved the complementary function. If a periodic disturbing force is applied to an oscillating mass then a particular integral must also be used.

4.   (a)   Find the general solution of the differential equation

$$\frac{d^2x}{dt^2} + 6\frac{dx}{dt} + 13x = 10 \sin 2t$$

     (b)   Comment on the significance of the particular integral.

Miscellaneous exercise

Formulation is the part of the modelling cycle where the main features of a situation are identified, simplications and assumptions are made and variables are chosen and connected with equations. This exercise will give you some experience of formulating differential equations as well as practice in solving the equations using the methods of this unit.

After working through this unit, you should appreciate that differential equations can be used as models to represent a vast range of real problems.

1. The freezing over of a pond roughly satisfies the following law of ice formation: the rate at which the thickness of ice increases is inversely proportional to the thickness of the ice.

    (a) In terms of a constant of proportionality k, set up and solve a differential equation for ice formation.

    (b) To be safe for skating, the ice on a village pond needs to be 3 cm thick. After one hour of freezing weather, the ice is only 1 cm thick. How much longer do you need to wait? Comment on the validity of your solution.

2. 50 litres of paint have been made up in a tank by mixing blue and yellow paint in the ratio 3 : 2. To produce tins of paint of various shades of green, this mixture is pumped out at 5 litres per minute whilst blue and yellow paint are mixed into the contents of the tank at rates of 2 and 3 litres per minute respectively.

    (a) Given that there are x litres of blue paint in the tank after t minutes, explain why
    $\frac{dx}{dt} = 2 - 0.1x$.

    (b) Find at what time the tank contains equal quantities of blue and yellow paint.

    (c) Comment on the validity of your solution.

3. During research into the spread of bacteria in a culture medium, it has been found that the rate at which the bacteria spread is proportional to the product of the areas of the affected and unaffected parts of the medium.

    (a) Given that a culture medium has unit area, set up a differential equation in x, the area affected. Show that

    $$\frac{x}{1-x} = Ae^{kt}$$

    where A and k are constants.

    (b) Half the culture medium is initially affected, whereas $\frac{2}{3}$ of the medium is affected after 24 hours. What proportion is affected after 48 hours?

4.   After many years of successful sheep farming on the moors above Caldale, a farmer's flock becomes infected with disease. This causes the death rate of sheep to exceed the birth rate by about 5% of the flock.

(a)   Set up a suitable differential equation to model this situation. Use your solution to describe what will happen to the size of the flock.

(b)   The owner buys 50 sheep a year to help maintain the flock. Modify your model and use your new solution to describe how the size of the flock will change over time.

5.   A chemical reaction involves two substances A and B which combine to form a third substance, C. Suppose that, initially, there are a grams of A and b grams of B. Then, at a later time t, there are $a - N$ grams of A, $b - N$ grams of B and $2N$ grams of C, where N satisfies the differential equation

$$\frac{dN}{dt} = k\,(a - N)(b - N), \text{ where } k \text{ is constant.}$$

(a)   In a particular reaction there are initially 50 grams of A and 60 grams of B. Find N at time t, given that $k = 0.001$.

(b)   What is the maximum amount of substance C that can form?

6.   If the price of a commodity increases, you would expect the demand to fall and vice versa. Economists often use a model in which

$$\frac{\text{proportional decrease in demand}}{\text{proportional increase in price}} = k$$

where k is a constant called the elasticity of demand. For example, if a price increase of 0.5% resulted in a 1% drop in demand, then k would be 2.

(a)   Justify the model

$$-\frac{P}{n}\frac{dn}{dP} = k$$

where n is the quantity of a commodity sold over some fixed period of time if the price is P. Solve this differential equation in terms of k.

(b)   Describe the effect on the total revenue (price x demand) of altering the price, for

$k < 1$ (inelastic demand)
$k = 1$
$k > 1$ (elastic demand)

7E. In one kind of car compass in common use, the rotation of the north marker is governed by the equation

$$I \frac{d^2\theta}{dt^2} = -n^2 \sin\theta - 2\mu \left(\frac{d\theta}{dt} - \frac{d\phi}{dt} \right)$$

where θ and ϕ denote the angles that the north marker and the car are currently pointing east of north, and n, I and μ are physical constants.

Show that when θ is small, the equation for θ is approximately

$$\frac{d^2\theta}{dt^2} + 2\lambda \frac{d\theta}{dt} + k^2 \theta = 2\lambda \frac{d\phi}{dt} \quad ①$$

where λ and k are constants which you should express in terms of μ, n and I. You are given that the design of the compass is such that $\mu = \sqrt{(n^2 I)}$. Show that $\lambda = k$.

The car is travelling steadily north along a straight road, and the compass is locked with the north marker pointing θ_0 east of north. If the compass is then unlocked, solve the above equation for θ in terms of t, the time from the instant of unlocking.

Some time later, after the compass has reached equilibrium, the car negotiates a right - angle bend in which the car's angle of travel east of north is

$$\phi(t) = \begin{cases} 0 & t < 0 \\ \dfrac{\pi t}{2T} & 0 \leq t \leq T \\ \dfrac{\pi}{2} & t > T \end{cases}$$

where t now denotes the time after reaching the bend.

Solve the differential equation ① for $0 \leq t \leq T$. Verify that $\frac{d\theta}{dt} \geq 0$ and hence show that $0 \leq \theta \leq \frac{\pi}{kT}$ for $0 \leq t \leq T$.

Hence explain why this solution will be a good approximation to the true angle θ of the north marker if $kT > 10\,\pi$.

[SMP]

61

SOLUTIONS

1 Review

1.1 The order of a differential equation

> If $y = x^3 - 5x^2 - 4x + 20$, find:
>
> (a) $\dfrac{d^3 y}{dx^3}$ (b) $\dfrac{d^4 y}{dx^4}$

(a) $\dfrac{dy}{dx} = 3x^2 - 10x - 4$ $\dfrac{d^2 y}{dx^2} = 6x - 10$ $\dfrac{d^3 y}{dx^3} = 6$

(b) $\dfrac{d^4 y}{dx^4} = 0$

> What is $f^{(4)}(t)$ if $f(t) = 3 \sin 2t$?

$f^{(3)}(t) = -24 \cos 2t \implies f^{(4)}(t) = 48 \sin 2t$

> What is the order of each of the differential equations above?

(a)   1   (b)   2   (c)   2

(d)   2   (e)   3   (f)   3

1.2 Solution by inspection

> (a)   Find the value of c for the particular solution curve that passes through the point $(1, 3)$.
>
> (b)   Sketch the family of solution curves.

(a) $y = x^3 + x + c$

     $\Rightarrow 3 = 1 + 1 + c$

     $\Rightarrow c = 1$

(b)

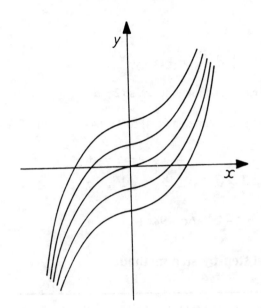

Exercise 1

1. (a) $y = x^2 - 3x + c$ (b) $y = c - x^2$

    (c) $s = c - \dfrac{1}{t}$ (d) $x = \sin 2t + c$

    (e) $y = c - \dfrac{2}{x}$ (f) $s = 3e^t + c$

    (g) $y = 2\sqrt{x} + c$ (h) $y = \dfrac{1}{4}x^4 + cx + d$

    (i) $s = -\sin t + ct + d$ (j) $x = -\dfrac{1}{4}\sin 2t + ct + d$

2. $y = \dfrac{1}{3}x^3 - 2x + c$

    (a) $5 = \dfrac{1}{3} \times 27 - 6 + c \Rightarrow c = 2$

    $y = \dfrac{1}{3}x^3 - 2x + 2$

    (b) $3 = \dfrac{1}{3} \times 125 - 10 + c \Rightarrow c = -28\dfrac{2}{3}$

    $y = \dfrac{1}{3}x^3 - 2x - 28\dfrac{2}{3}$

3. $x = \dfrac{1}{3}\sin 3t + c$

    (a) $0 = 0 + c \Rightarrow c = 0$

    $x = \dfrac{1}{3}\sin 3t$

    (b) $1 = \dfrac{1}{3}\sin\dfrac{3\pi}{6} + c \Rightarrow c = \dfrac{2}{3}$

    $x = \dfrac{1}{3}\sin 3t + \dfrac{2}{3}$

65

4. $\frac{dy}{dx} = x^3 - x^2 - x + c$

$y = \frac{1}{4}x^4 - \frac{1}{3}x^3 - \frac{1}{2}x^2 + cx + d$

The curve passes through (0, 2), so $2 = d$

The curve passes through (4, 4) so $4 = 64 - \frac{1}{3} \times 64 - 8 + 4c + 2$

$$\Rightarrow c = -8\frac{1}{6}$$

$$y = \frac{1}{4}x^4 - \frac{1}{3}x^3 - \frac{1}{2}x^2 - 8\frac{1}{6}x + 2$$

$$\Rightarrow 12y = 3x^4 - 4x^3 - 6x^2 - 98x + 24$$

1.3 A numerical step-by-step method

> (a) Continue the table to obtain an estimate of y when $x = 1.5$.
>
> (b) Use a suitable program to check your results for the table above, and extend it to $x = 2.0$.
>
> Also (if possible) check your results using a solution sketching program.

(a)

x	y	$\frac{dy}{dx}$	dx	dy	$x + dx$	$y + dy$
1.2	3.863	5.32	0.1	0.532	1.3	4.395
1.3	4.395	6.07	0.1	0.607	1.4	5.002
1.4	5.002	6.88	0.1	0.688	1.5	5.690
1.5	5.690					

(b) When $x = 2.0$, $y = 10.555$

> (a) With the aid of a sketch, explain why the step-by-step method in the example above underestimates the actual value.
>
> (b) Investigate how the error is affected by varying the step size.

(a)

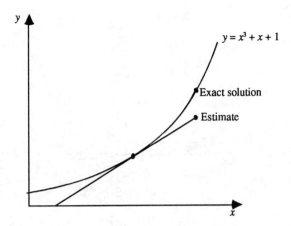

For $x > 0$, $3x^2 + 1$ increases as x increases. The curve is therefore concave up and the tangent at any point lies below the curve. The numerical solution at any value of x will therefore always be less than the exact value.

(b) The table below illustrates how accuracy increases as the step size is reduced.

dx	x	y	error
0.5	1.5	5.000	0.875
0.25	1.5	5.422	0.453
0.1	1.5	5.690	0.185
0.05	1.5	5.782	0.093
0.01	1.5	5.856	0.019

The exact value is
$y = 5.875$ when $x = 1.5$

Exercise 2

1.   (a, b) For integer values of x, the numerical solutions are as follows:

x	y	y	y	y	y
−3.0	2.0	2.25	2.05	1.95	1.75
−2.0	1.0	1.6	1.1	0.9	0.4
−1.0	0.0	1.3	0.3	− 0.3	− 1.3
0.0	−1.0	1.8	−0.4	− 1.6	− 3.8
1.0	−2.0	4.4	−0.7	− 3.3	− 8.4
2.0	−3.0	11.4	−0.1	− 5.9	−17.4
3.0	−4.0	28.4	2.5	−10.5	−36.4

(c)

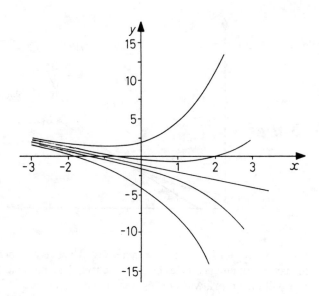

(d) For large negative x, the curves become asymptotic to the line $y + x + 1 = 0$.

The differential equation $\frac{dy}{dx} = x + y$ has exact solution $y = ce^x - x - 1$. This can be confirmed by differentiation:

$$\frac{dy}{dx} = ce^x - 1$$

$$= (y + x + 1) - 1$$

$$= y + x$$

$c = 0$ gives the equation of the line $y + x + 1 = 0$, which is the solution curve through $(-3, 2)$.

2.

t	0	0.2	0.4	0.6	0.8	1.0	1.2	1.4	1.6	1.8	2.0
v	15	12.5	11.4	10.8	10.5	10.3	10.2	10.1	10.1	10.0	10.0

The parachutist has slowed down and reached her terminal velocity. Descent will continue at a steady 10 ms⁻¹.

3. Using $dp = 0.1$, an approximate value of 3450 is obtained for n when $p = 12$.

The exact solution is $n = \dfrac{10^6}{2p^2}$, which gives $n \approx 3472$ when $p = 12$.

2 *Numerical solutions*

2.1 Parametric equations

> Complete the table to obtain an estimate of the
> position of the point of connection when $t = 1.0$.

t	x	y	dt	dx	dy
0	3.0	4.0	0.2	0.8	–0.6
0.2	3.8	3.4	0.2	0.66	–0.75
0.4	4.46	2.65	0.2	0.50	–0.86
0.6	4.97	1.79	0.2	0.32	–0.95
0.8	5.29	0.84	0.2	0.13	–0.99
1.0	5.42	–0.15			

When $t = 1$, the position is approximately $(5.42, -0.15)$.

2.2 Simultaneous linear equations

> (a)   If $x = 3$ and $y = 4$ when $t = 0$, find the exact solution
> of these two differential equations.
>
> (b)   What is the shape of a graph of y against x?

(a) $x = 4 \sin t + 3 \cos t + c \implies x = 4 \sin t + 3 \cos t$

$\quad\quad y = -3 \sin t + 4 \cos t + d \implies y = -3 \sin t + 4 \cos t$

(b) $x^2 + y^2 = 25 \sin^2 t + 25 \cos^2 t \implies x^2 + y^2 = 25$.

The path is a circle of radius 5, with centre the origin.

Exercise 1

1.   (a)

t	0	1.0	2.0	3.0	4.0	5.0
x	70	75.4	77.1	77.6	77.7	77.8
y	30	24.6	22.9	22.4	22.3	22.2

x	90	81.5	78.9	78.1	77.9	77.8
y	10	18.5	21.1	21.9	22.1	22.2

(c)

x	10	57.3	71.6	75.9	77.2	77.6
y	90	42.7	28.4	24.1	22.8	22.4

For $t > 5$, a steady state with $x \approx 78$ and $y \approx 22$ appears to be reached.

These simultaneous differential equations have a symbolic solution:

$$x = \frac{10}{9}(70 - Ae^{-0.5t})$$
$$y = \frac{10}{9}(20 + Ae^{-0.5t})$$

As $t \to +\infty$, $x \to 77.\dot{7}$ and $y \to 22.\dot{2}$

2. (a)

t	0	0.2	0.4	0.6	0.8	1.0
x	3	3.80	4.48	5.01	5.36	5.51
y	4	3.40	2.64	1.74	0.74	−0.33

(b) It is easy to check that

$$x = 3 \cos t + 4 \sin t$$
$$y = -3\sin t + 4 \cos t$$

satisfy both sets of differential equations.

The point (x, y) therefore lies on the circle $x^2 + y^2 = 25$. The numerical solution is not very accurate because the value of x becomes greater than 5.

3. (a)

t	0	1	2	3	4	5
i	0	−0.7	−1.3	−2.0	−2.7	−3.5
q	0	1.3	2.3	3.1	3.8	4.3

(b)

t	0	1	2	3	4	5
i	0	1.0	0.8	0.6	0.4	0.3
q	0	0.9	1.8	2.4	2.9	3.3

A symbolic solution for these equations gives $i = 0.32$ and $q = 3.28$ (to 2 decimal places), when $t = 5$. The solution with $dt = 0.5$ is therefore very inaccurate.

Solution curves (with $dt = 0.1$) are:

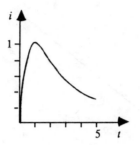 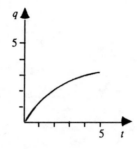

4E.

t	0	0.1	0.2	0.3	0.4	0.5
u	110	112	114.4	117.3	120.7	124.9
v	90	88	85.6	82.7	79.3	75.1
w	100	120	140	160	180	200

t	0.6	0.7	0.8	0.9	1.0
u	129.9	135.8	143.0	151.6	161.9
v	70.1	64.2	57.0	48.4	38.1
w	220	240	260	280	300

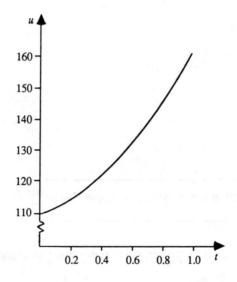 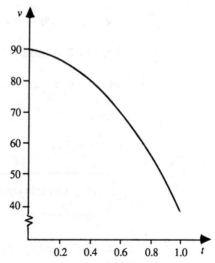

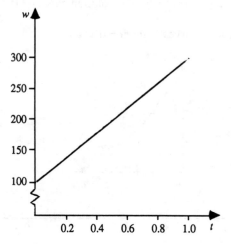

At $t = 1$, $(u, v, w) \approx (162, 38, 300)$.

It is clear that u and w increase as v decreases. Furthermore, $u + v = 200$.

2.3   Second order linear equations

> For the differential equation $\dfrac{d^2y}{dt^2} = -10$, suppose $y = 7$
>
> and $\dfrac{dy}{dt} = 3$ when $t = 0$. Find y when $t = 4$.

$\dfrac{dy}{dt} = -10t + c, \ y = -5t^2 + ct + d$

$\dfrac{dy}{dt} = 3$ when $t = 0$ and so $c = 3$.

$y \ = 7$ when $t = 0$ and so $d = 7$.

$y \ = -5t^2 + 3t + 7$.

$y \ = -61$ when $t = 4$.

> Why can this equation not be solved by inspection?

$\dfrac{dv}{dt} = -x$ cannot be solved by inspection, as the derivative is expressed as a function of x and not of t.

> **Explain each term in this expression and show why the equation of motion has this form.**

x stands for the displacement of the object from the source of attraction.

$m \dfrac{d^2x}{dt^2}$ is mass x acceleration. From Newton's second law, this equals the total force.

The resisting force due to air resistance is of the form $-A\dfrac{dx}{dt}$, where $\dfrac{dx}{dt}$ is the velocity and A is a constant.

The returning force to the source of attraction is of the form $-Bx$, where B is a constant.

Then $m\dfrac{d^2x}{dt^2} = -A\dfrac{dx}{dt} - Bx \Rightarrow m\dfrac{d^2x}{dt^2} + A\dfrac{dx}{dt} + Bx = 0.$

Exercise 2

1. (a) Let $v = \dfrac{dy}{dx}$, then

$$\frac{dv}{dx} = 4 - 9y \quad \text{and} \quad \frac{dy}{dx} = v$$

Using a step of $dx = 0.1$, the following points are obtained.

x	5	5.5	6.0	6.5	7.0	7.5	8.0	8.5	9.0	9.5	10.0
y	0	0.8	1.2	0.1	−0.85	0.6	2.5	0.8	−2.6	−1.0	4.7
v	1	1.8	−1.0	−3.0	0.7	4.9	0.2	−7.4	−2.4	10.8	6.8

(b)

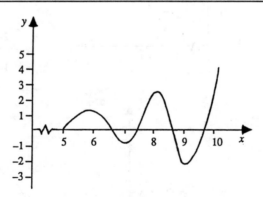

2. Let $v = \dfrac{dx}{dt}$, then

$$\frac{dv}{dt} = 1 - 0.8v + 3.2x \quad \text{and} \quad v = \frac{dx}{dt}$$

Using $dt = 0.1$:

t	0	0.5	1	1.5	2	2.5	3
x	2	2.7	5.1	10.2	20.2	39.8	78.0
v	0	3.4	7.5	15.0	29.4	57.4	112.2

The estimated speed is 112 ms⁻¹.

73

3. $\dfrac{di}{dt} = 7.3 - 5.4q - 9.4i$ and $i = \dfrac{dq}{dt}$

Using $dt = 0.1$, the following results are obtained:

t	0	0.5	1	1.5	2
q	0	0.29	0.58	0.79	0.94
i	0	0.65	0.47	0.34	0.25

The estimated current is 0.25 amps.

4E. (a) $dy = 0.5$, $dx = \dfrac{0.5}{z^2}$ and $dz = 0.5x$

x	1	1.5	1.72	1.82	1.87	1.90	1.92	1.94	1.95
y	1	1.5	2.0	2.5	3.0	3.5	4.0	4.5	5.0
z	1	1.5	2.25	3.11	4.02	4.96	5.91	6.87	7.84

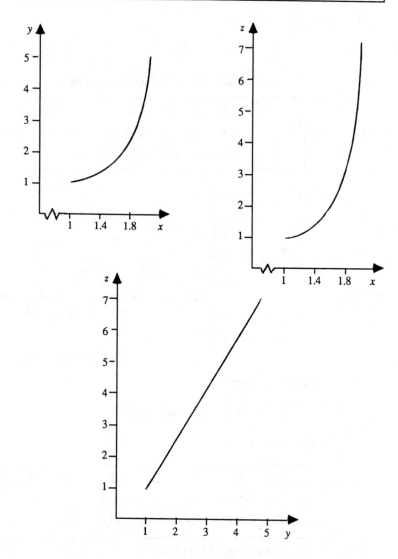

74

(b) $dx = 0.5$, $dy = 0.5z^2$ and $dz = 0.5xz^2$

x	1	1.5	2.0	2.5	3.0	3.5	4.0
y	1	1.5	2.6	7.7	96.8	27956	3.5×10^9
z	1	1.5	3.2	13.35	236.0	83814	1.2×10^{10}

The numerical solution diverges rapidly. You can have no confidence in the accuracy of the solution.

5E.   Let $v = \dfrac{dx}{dt}$ and $y = \dfrac{d^2x}{dt^2}$. For $dt = 0.5$, $dx = 0.5v$, $dv = 0.5y$ and $dy = 1.5 + y$.

t	0	1	2	3	4	5
x	0	1.25	15.6	87	390.9	1629.25
v	0	8.25	45.75	200.25	822.75	3317.25
y	5	24.5	102.5	414.5	1662.5	6654.5

When $t = 5$, $x \approx 1629$ and $\dfrac{dx}{dt} \approx 3317$. However, the solution is diverging rapidly and so you can have no confidence in these results.

3 First order equations

3.1 Separable variables

(a) $\dfrac{1}{y^2}\,dy = x\,dx$

$\displaystyle\int \dfrac{1}{y^2}\,dy = \int x\,dx$

$-\dfrac{1}{y} = \dfrac{1}{2}x^2 + c$

$y = \dfrac{-2}{x^2 + 2c}$

(b) $\displaystyle\int \dfrac{1}{y^2 + 1}\,dy = \int x\,dx$

$\tan^{-1} y = \dfrac{1}{2}x^2 + c$

$y = \tan\left(\dfrac{1}{2}x^2 + c\right)$

(c) $dy = (y^2 x + 1)\,dx$

The equation cannot be separated into y terms on one side and x terms on the other.

(a) As $t \to +\infty$, $v \to 10$. The terminal velocity of the stone is 10 ms^{-1}.

(b) A is determined by the initial or **boundary** conditions. For example, if $v = 2$ ms^{-1} initially, then $2 = 10 - Ae^{-0}$. Therefore $A = 8$ and the solution is $v = 10 - 8e^{-t}$.

(c)
$$v = 10 - Ae^{-t}$$

$$\frac{dv}{dt} = Ae^{-t}$$

$$\Rightarrow v + \frac{dv}{dt} = 10$$

$$\Rightarrow \frac{dv}{dt} = 10 - v, \text{ as required.}$$

Exercise 1

1. (a) $\int \frac{1}{y^2} dy = \int dx$

$$-\frac{1}{y} = x + c$$

$$y = -\frac{1}{x+c}$$

(b) $\int \frac{1}{y} dy = \int dx$

$$\ln y = x + c$$

$$y = e^{x+c}$$

$$y = e^c e^x$$

$$y = Ae^x$$

(c) $y = Ae^{3x}$

(d) $y = 1 + Ae^{-\frac{1}{x}}$

2. (a) $\frac{1}{y} dy = -2x dx$

$$\ln y = -x^2 + c$$

$$y = e^{-x^2+c} = e^c e^{-x^2}$$

$$y = Ae^{-x^2}$$

(b) At $(0,4)$, $4 = Ae^0 = A$

The particular solution is $y = 4e^{-x^2}$.

3. (a) $y = \frac{7}{5} + Be^{-5x}$

(b) Not possible using separable variables.

(c) $\int y \, dy = \int (10 - x) \, dx$

$$y^2 = d + 20x - x^2$$

(d) $\sqrt{y} = \frac{x\sqrt{x}}{3} + c$

4. $r^2\dfrac{dV}{dr} = K$

$$\int dV = \int \dfrac{K}{r^2}\, dr$$

$$V = -\dfrac{K}{r} + c$$

At $r = 5$, $\qquad 40 = -\dfrac{1}{5}K + c$

At $r = 3$, $\qquad 0 = -\dfrac{1}{3}K + c$

$$\Rightarrow\ 40 = \left(\dfrac{1}{3} - \dfrac{1}{5}\right)K$$

$$\Rightarrow\ K = 300$$

Then $\quad c = 100$

The general expression for the potential is $100 - \dfrac{300}{r}$ volts.

5E. (a) $\qquad v\dfrac{dv}{ds} = -\dfrac{gr^2}{s^2}$

$$\Rightarrow \int v\, dv = -gr^2 \int \dfrac{1}{s^2}\, ds$$

$$\Rightarrow \quad \dfrac{v^2}{2} = \dfrac{gr^2}{s} + c$$

When $s = r$, $\qquad \dfrac{u^2}{2} = gr + c$

So $\dfrac{v^2}{2} = \dfrac{gr^2}{s} + \dfrac{u^2}{2} - gr$

$$\Rightarrow v^2 = u^2 - 2gr\left(1 - \dfrac{r}{s}\right)$$

(b) $\qquad 0 = 5600^2 - 2 \times 9.8 \times 6.4 \times 10^6 \left(1 - \dfrac{6.4 \times 10^6}{s}\right)$

$$\Rightarrow \dfrac{1}{4} = 1 - \dfrac{6.4 \times 10^6}{s}$$

$$\Rightarrow s \approx 8.5 \times 10^6$$

(c) The rocket rises to a distance of approximately 8.5×10^6 m from the centre of the Earth before starting to descend.

(d) If $s \to +\infty$, then $v^2 \to u^2 - 2gr$

Therefore $u^2 \geq 2gr$

$$\Rightarrow u^2 \geq 2 \times 9.8 \times 6.4 \times 10^6$$

The initial speed is at least $11\ 200$ ms^{-1}.

78

3.2 Particular integrals

(a) For the depth of liquid during the scrubbing out process, justify the model

$$\frac{dy}{dt} + 0.01y = 0.5$$

Obtain a symbolic solution.

(b) What constant value of y is a solution of the differential equation?

(c) Obtain a symbolic solution for the situation when the water jets are switched off.

(d) How do the solutions in (b) and (c) relate to that for (a)?

(a) If the water jets are switched off, then the model suggested is

$$\frac{dy}{dt} = -0.01y$$

This fits the data reasonably well. For example, at $t = 0$,

$$dt = 5 \implies dy = -25.$$

On the curve, the change in y is -26.

With the jets on,

$$\frac{dy}{dt} = -0.01y + 0.5$$

$$\implies \frac{dy}{dt} + 0.01y = 0.5$$

The equation can also be rearranged into a separated variables form:

$$\int \frac{dy}{0.5 - 0.01y} = \int dt$$

$$-\frac{1}{0.01} \ln(0.5 - 0.01y) = t + d$$

$$0.5 - 0.01y = Ae^{-0.01t}$$

$$y = 50 + Be^{-0.01t}$$

(b) If y is constant, then $\frac{dy}{dt} = 0$ and

$$0.01y = 0.5$$
$$\Rightarrow \quad y = 50$$

When the depth of liquid is 50 cm, the amounts flowing in and out are equal and so the level remains constant. From (a), it can be seen that the water level tends exponentially to 50 cm.

(c) $\quad \frac{dy}{dt} = -0.01y$

$$\Rightarrow y = Ae^{-0.01t}$$

(d) The general solution appears to be the sum of the particular integral $y = 50$ and the general solution for

$$\frac{dy}{dt} + 0.01y = 0$$

This important idea is investigated further in this chapter.

Exercise 2

1. (a) 3

   (b) $2t - 1$

   (c) $2t + 2$

   (d) $\frac{1}{4} - \frac{1}{2}t + \frac{1}{2}t^2$

   (e) $-\frac{3}{4} + \frac{3}{2}t + \frac{1}{2}t^2$

   (f) $-\frac{15}{4} + \frac{3}{2}t + \frac{1}{2}t^2$

2. A particular integral for

$$\frac{dx}{dt} + 2x = f(t) + g(t)$$

can be obtained by adding the particular integrals for

$$\frac{dx}{dt} + 2x = f(t) \text{ and } \frac{dx}{dt} + 2x = g(t)$$

A particular integral for $\frac{dx}{dt} + 2x = t^2 - 4t + 6$ is therefore

$$\frac{1}{4} - \frac{1}{2}t + \frac{1}{2}t^2 - (2t - 1) + 3$$

$$= \frac{17}{4} - \frac{5}{2}t + \frac{1}{2}t^2$$

3.   (a) $y = 3$

     (b) $v = 6r - 15$

     (c) $p = 16y^2 - 80y + 200$

     (d) $h = 3 + (6t - 15) + 16t^2 - 80t + 200$

          $= 16t^2 - 74t + 188$

4.   (a) $-14.6\,e^{2t}$

     (b) $-e^{-4x}$

     (c) $0.16 \sin 4s - 0.32 \cos 4s$

     (d) $2 \sin 3z - \cos 3z$

5.   (a) $\frac{1}{3} e^{5t}$

     (b) $-0.1 \sin 4t - 0.2 \cos 4t$

     (c) $3(-0.1 \sin 4t - 0.2 \cos 4t) + 6(\frac{1}{3} e^{5t})$

          $= -0.3 \sin 4t - 0.6 \cos 4t + 2e^{5t}$

3.3   Linear equations

Exercise 3

1.   (a) $CF = Ae^{-3x}, \quad PI = 8$

          $y = Ae^{-3x} + 8$

          $y = 8 - 8e^{-3x}$

     (b) $CF = Ae^{-2x}, \quad PI = x - \frac{1}{2}$

          $y = Ae^{-2x} + x - \frac{1}{2}$

          $y = \frac{1}{2} e^{-2x} + x - \frac{1}{2}$

     (c) $CF = Ae^{-2x}, \quad PI = -3\frac{1}{2}$

          $y = Ae^{-2x} - 3\frac{1}{2}$

          $y = 3\frac{1}{2}(e^{-2x} - 1)$

     (d) $CF = Ae^{-2x}, \quad PI = x - \frac{1}{2} - 3\frac{1}{2} = x - 4$

          $y = Ae^{-2x} + x - 4$

          $y = 4e^{-2x} + x - 4$

2.   (a) $y = Ae^{2x} - 6$

     (b) $y = Ae^{-8t} + 1.25$

     (c) $P = Ae^{-3t}$

     (d) $V = Ae^h + 5h$

     (e) $y = Ae^{-2x} + \dfrac{1}{3} e^x$

3E. (a)   For any value of K,

           $$\frac{d}{dx}\left(Ke^{4x}\right) - 4\left(Ke^{4x}\right) = 0$$

     (b) $Ke^{4x} + 4Kxe^{4x} - 4Kxe^{4x} = 3e^{4x}$

           $$\Rightarrow K = 3$$

           A general solution is $Ae^{4x} + 3xe^{4x}$.

     (c)   (i) $Ae^{-2x} + xe^{-2x}$

           (ii) $Ae^{6x} + 3xe^{6x}$

4 Second order equations

4.3 The auxiliary equation

> **Under what circumstances would the auxiliary equation method *not* produce a complementary function with two arbitrary constants?**

- The equation $am^2 + bm + c = 0$ would have no real roots if $b^2 < 4ac$.

- It would have just one (repeated) root if $b^2 = 4ac$.

Both of these cases are dealt with later in this chapter.

4.4 General solutions

Exercise 1

1. $CF = Ae^{2x} + Be^{3x}$

   Substituting $y = Ke^x$ in the differential equation,

   $$K - 5K + 6K = 1 \Rightarrow K = \frac{1}{2}$$

   $PI = \frac{1}{2} e^x$

   The general solution is $y = Ae^{2x} + Be^{3x} + \frac{1}{2} e^x$

2. The auxiliary equation is $\quad m^2 - 3m + 2 = 0$
   $$\Leftrightarrow (m-1)(m-2) = 0$$

   $CF = Ae^t + Be^{2t}$

   Substituting $x = at + b$ in the differential equation,

   $$-3a + 2at + 2b = 4t$$

   So $a = 2$ and $b = 3$

   $PI = 2t + 3$

   The general solution is $x = Ae^t + Be^{2t} + 2t + 3$

Differentiating, $\frac{dx}{dt} = Ae^t + 2Be^{2t} + 2$

Since $x = 5$ and $\frac{dx}{dt} = 3$ when $t = 0$,

$$5 = A + B + 3$$
$$\text{and } 3 = A + 2B + 2$$

Hence $B = -1$ and $A = 3$ and the required solution is $x = 3e^t - e^{2t} + 2t + 3$

3.   The auxiliary equation is $m^2 = 0$ which has 0 as a repeated root. However, the equation can be integrated directly.

$$\frac{dx}{dt} = 2t^2 + c$$
$$\Rightarrow x = \frac{2}{3}t^3 + ct + d$$

The particular solution is $x = \frac{2}{3}t^3 + 3t + 5$.

4. $$m^2 + 3m - 10 = 0$$
$$\Rightarrow (m - 2)(m + 5) = 0$$
$$y = Ae^{2x} + Be^{-5x}$$

5.   (a) $$m^2 - 4m + 3 = 0$$
$$\Rightarrow (m - 1)(m - 3) = 0$$
$$y = Ae^x + Be^{3x}$$

   (b)   If $y = ax + b$, $-4a + 3(ax + b) = 6x - 8$
$$\Rightarrow a = 2, b = 0$$

$$y = Ae^x + Be^{3x} + 2x$$

6. $$m^2 - 4 = 0$$
$$\Rightarrow (m - 2)(m + 2) = 0$$

$$y = Ae^{2x} + Be^{-2x}$$

When $x = 0$, $A + B = 2$ and $2A - 2B = 2$
$$\Rightarrow A = \frac{3}{2}, B = \frac{1}{2}$$
$$y = \frac{3}{2}e^{2x} + \frac{1}{2}e^{-2x}$$

7. $$CF = Ae^{-x} + Be^{-3x}$$

$$PI = \frac{1}{2}e^x$$

$$y = Ae^{-x} + Be^{-3x} + \frac{1}{2}e^x$$

4.5 Substitution

Exercise 2

1. $\frac{dz}{dx} + z = 3x - 1$

$$z = Ae^{-x} + 3x - 4$$

$$\frac{dy}{dx} - 3y = Ae^{-x} + 3x - 4$$

$$y = Be^{3x} + \frac{1}{2}Ae^{-x} - x + 1$$

$$y = Be^{3x} + Ce^{-x} - x + 1$$

2. $\frac{dz}{dx} + z = 2\sin x$

$$z = Ae^{-x} + \sin x - \cos x$$

$$\frac{dy}{dx} - y = Ae^{-x} + \sin x - \cos x$$

When $x = 0$, $-1 = A - 1 \Rightarrow A = 0$

$$\frac{dy}{dx} - y = \sin x - \cos x$$

$$y = Be^{x} - \sin x$$

When $x = 0$, $1 = B$

$$y = e^{x} - \sin x$$

3E. $\frac{dy}{dx} = z + x\frac{dz}{dx}$

$$z + x\frac{dz}{dx} = z + x^2$$

$$x\frac{dz}{dx} = x^2$$

$$\frac{dz}{dx} = x$$

$$z = \frac{1}{2}x^2 + c$$

$$y = \frac{1}{2}x^3 + cx$$

4E. $y = z^2 \Rightarrow \frac{dy}{dx} = 2z\frac{dz}{dx}$

$$2z\frac{dz}{dx} + 2z^2 = 4z$$

$$\Rightarrow \quad \frac{dz}{dx} + z = 2$$

$$\Rightarrow \quad z = Ae^{-x} + 2$$

$$\Rightarrow \quad y = (Ae^{-x} + 2)^2$$

Since $y = 0$ when $x = 0$, $A = -2$ and $y = 4(1 - e^{-x})^2$.

4.6   Equal roots

> **Carry out the auxiliary equation method for**
>
> $$\frac{d^2y}{dx^2} + 4\frac{dy}{dx} + 4y = 0$$
>
> **and justify the statement above.**

The auxiliary equation is

$$m^2 + 4m + 4 = 0$$
$$\Rightarrow (m + 2)(m + 2) = 0$$

A complementary function of the form

$$Ae^{-2x} + Be^{-2x}$$

is simply Ce^{-2x} for $C = A + B$. This function therefore has only one arbitrary constant.

Exercise 3

1. $\quad m^2 - 2m + 1 = 0$
    $\Rightarrow (m - 1)(m - 1) = 0$

    $CF = (Ax + B)e^x$
    $PI = 7$
    $y = (Ax + B)e^x + 7$

2. The auxiliary equation is $m^2 + 6m + 9 = 0$
    $\qquad\qquad\qquad\qquad\qquad \Rightarrow (m + 3)(m + 3) = 0$

    $CF = (Ax + B)e^{-3x}$
    $PI = \dfrac{1}{9}x - \dfrac{2}{27}$
    $y = (Ax + B)e^{-3x} + \dfrac{1}{9}x - \dfrac{2}{27}$

3. $\quad 16m^2 + 8m + 1 = 0$
    $\Rightarrow (4m + 1)(4m + 1) = 0$

    $y = (Ax + B)e^{-\frac{1}{4}x}$

4. $\quad m^2 - 10m + 25 = 0$
    $\Rightarrow (m - 5)(m - 5) = 0$

    $CF = (Ax + B)e^{5x}$
    $PI = e^{2x}$
    $y = (Ax + B)e^{5x} + e^{2x}$
    When $x = 0$, $y = 0 \Rightarrow B = -1$ and $\dfrac{dy}{dx} = 0 \Rightarrow A = 3$
    $y = (3x - 1)e^{5x} + e^{2x}$

5. If $y = Ae^{2x}$, $\frac{dy}{dx} = 2Ae^{2x}$ and $\frac{d^2y}{dx^2} = 4Ae^{2x}$.

Then $(4 - 14 + 10)Ae^{2x} = e^{2x}$

$\Rightarrow$ $0 = e^{2x}$

This is not true and so there is no PI of the form Ae^{2x}.

If $y = Axe^{2x}$, $\frac{dy}{dx} = Ae^{2x} + 2Axe^{2x}$

and $\frac{d^2y}{dx^2} = 4Ae^{2x} + 4Axe^{2x}$

Then $(4 - 7)Ae^{2x} = e^{2x}$

$\Rightarrow$ $A = -\frac{1}{3}$

$-\frac{1}{3}xe^{2x}$ is a particular integral.

In this problem, one of the roots of the auxiliary equation is 2 and this makes it impossible to obtain a PI of the form Ae^{2x}. However, the idea of considering Axe^{2x} was successful. It is interesting that this is the same idea as is used for the CF when the auxiliary equation has a repeated root.

4.7 Complex roots

Exercise 4

1. (a) The auxiliary equation is $m^2 - 2m + 2 = 0$

    $\Leftrightarrow m = \frac{2 \pm \sqrt{(4 - 8)}}{2}$

    $\Leftrightarrow m = 1 \pm j$

    $y = e^x (A \sin x + B \cos x)$

    (b) Try a particular integral of the form $Cx + D$.

    $-2C + 2(Cx + D) = x$

    $\Rightarrow 2C = 1$, $-2C + 2D = 0$

    $\Rightarrow C = \frac{1}{2}$, $D = \frac{1}{2}$

    $y = Ae^x \sin x + Be^x \cos x + \frac{1}{2}x + \frac{1}{2}$

2. CF $= A \cos t + B \sin t$
    PI $= t$

The general solution is $x = A \cos t + B \sin t + t$

$$\Rightarrow \frac{dx}{dt} = -A \sin t + B \cos t + 1$$

When $t = 0$, $0 = A$

$$2 = B + 1 \Rightarrow B = 1$$

The particular solution is $x = \sin t + t$.

3E. The auxiliary equation is $m^2 + 2m + 10 = 0$

$$\Leftrightarrow m = \frac{-2 \pm \sqrt{(4-40)}}{2}$$

$$\Leftrightarrow m = -1 \pm 3j$$

The complementary function is $e^{-t}(A \cos 3t + B \sin 3t)$.

Try a particular integral of the form $C \cos t + D \sin t$.

$-C \cos t - D \sin t + 2(-C \sin t + D \cos t) + 10(C \cos t + D \sin t) = 2 \cos t + 9 \sin t$

$(-C + 2D + 10C) \cos t + (-D - 2C + 10D) \sin t = 2 \cos t + 9 \sin t$

$9C + 2D = 2,\ 9D - 2C = 9$

$$\Rightarrow C = 0,\ D = 1$$

$I = \sin t$ is a particular integral.

$$I = Ae^{-t} \cos 3t + Be^{-t} \sin 3t + \sin t.$$

$\frac{dI}{dt} = e^{-t}(-A \cos 3t - 3A \sin 3t - B \sin 3t + 3B \cos 3t) + \cos t$

When $t = 0$, $I = 0 \Rightarrow A = 0$

$$\frac{dI}{dt} = 0 \Rightarrow 3B + 1 = 0$$

$$\Rightarrow B = -\frac{1}{3}$$

The particular solution is $\sin t - \frac{1}{3} e^{-t} \sin 3t$.

At time t, the current is $\sin t - \frac{1}{3} e^{-t} \sin 3t$ amps.

Miscellaneous exercise

1.　(a)　For thickness x units, $\frac{dx}{dt} = \frac{k}{x}$.

So $\int x\,dx = \int k\,dt$

$\Rightarrow \quad \frac{1}{2}x^2 = kt + C$

(b)　Using units of centimetres and hours, $x = 0$ when $t = 0$ and $x = 1$ when $t = 1$.
Then $x^2 = t$ and so $x = 3$ when $t = 9$.

You must expect to wait a further 8 hours, although this depends upon the weather conditions remaining constant.

2.　(a)　Mixture is pumped out at 5 litres per minute and so blue paint is being pumped out at $\frac{x}{50} \times 5 = 0.1x$ litres per minute. Since it is being pumped in at 2 litres per minute, $\frac{dx}{dt} = 2 - 0.1x$.

(b)　$x = 20 + Ae^{-0.1t}$

$x = 30$ when $t = 0 \Rightarrow x = 20 + 10e^{-0.1t}$

Then $x = 25$ when $e^{-0.1t} = 0.5$
$$\Rightarrow t = -\frac{1}{0.1}\ln 0.5$$
$$\approx 6.9$$

The amounts are equal after 6.9 minutes.

(c)　The answer is likely to be inaccurate because it is based upon the assumption that the paint is perfectly mixed at all times. If the new paint is poured in at the top whilst the old paint is removed at the bottom with virtually no mixing, then it will take only 5 minutes for the amounts to become equal.

3.　(a)　The rate of spread is $\frac{dx}{dt}$ and so

$\frac{dx}{dt} = kx(1 - x)$, k constant.

$\int \frac{dx}{x(1-x)} = \int k\,dt$

$\Rightarrow \int \left(\frac{1}{x} + \frac{1}{1-x}\right) dx = \int k\,dt$

$\Rightarrow \ln x - \ln(1-x) = kt + c$

$\Rightarrow \qquad \ln \frac{x}{1-x} = kt + c$

$\Rightarrow \qquad \frac{x}{1-x} = e^{kt+c}$

$\Rightarrow \qquad \frac{x}{1-x} = Ae^{kt}$

(b) $t = 0$: $A = \frac{1}{2} + \frac{1}{2} = 1$

$t = 24$: $e^{24k} = \frac{2}{3} + \frac{1}{3} = 2$

When $t = 48$, $\frac{x}{1-x} = e^{48k} = 4$

$\Rightarrow x = \frac{4}{5}$

4.   Let P be the size of the flock. Assume P is sufficiently large that the (t, P) graph can be regarded as a smooth curve.

(a) $\frac{dP}{dt} = -0.05P$

$\Rightarrow P = Ae^{-0.05t}$

The size of the flock will drop exponentially to zero, from its initial size A.

(b)   The modified equation is $\frac{dP}{dt} = 50 - 0.05P$.

This is a first order linear equation with

$CF = Ae^{-0.05t}$ and $PI = 1000$

$P = Ae^{-0.05t} + 1000$

If nothing is done about the disease and if the birth and death rates remain constant, then the size of the flock tends to 1000, irrespective of the initial size.

5.   (a) $\frac{dN}{dt} = 0.001\,(50 - N)(60 - N)$

This is a separable differential equation, which can be integrated to give

$\ln\left(\frac{60-N}{50-N}\right) = 0.01t + C$

$\Rightarrow \frac{60-N}{50-N} = Ae^{0.01t}$

At $t = 0$, $N = 0$ and so $A = 1.2$

This leads to $N = \dfrac{60\,(1 - e^{0.01t})}{1 - 1.2e^{0.01t}}$

(b)   For the solution in (a), as $t \to +\infty$, $N \to \frac{60}{1.2} = 50$.

It is clear from the differential equation that the maximum value of N is 50. The reaction would then have to stop because none of substance A would be left. 100 grams is the maximum amount of C that can be formed

In general, the maximum amount of C that can be formed is twice the lesser of a and b.

6.   (a)   Proportional decrease in demand $= -\dfrac{dn}{n}$

            Proportional increase in price $= \dfrac{dP}{P}$

            So $k = -\dfrac{dn}{n} \div \dfrac{dP}{P} = -\dfrac{P}{n}\dfrac{dn}{dP}$

            Then $\dfrac{dn}{n} = -k\,\dfrac{dP}{P}$

                 $\ln n = -k \ln P + C$

                    $n = \dfrac{A}{P^k}$

   (b)   If $k < 1$, then the revenue, $\dfrac{A}{P^{k-1}}$, increases as the price increases.

            If $k = 1$, the revenue is A and is independent of the price.

            If $k > 1$, the revenue increases as the price drops.

7E.   For small θ, $\sin\theta \approx \theta$ and the differential equation can be written as

$$I\frac{d^2\theta}{dt^2} = -n^2\theta - 2\mu\left(\frac{d\theta}{dt} - \frac{d\phi}{dt}\right)$$

i.e. $\dfrac{d^2\theta}{dt^2} + 2\lambda\dfrac{d\theta}{dt} + k^2\theta = 2\lambda\dfrac{d\phi}{dt}$

where $\lambda = \dfrac{\mu}{I}$ and $k^2 = \dfrac{n^2}{I}$.

If $\mu = \sqrt{(n^2 I)}$, then $\lambda = \dfrac{\sqrt{(n^2 I)}}{I} = \sqrt{\left(\dfrac{n^2}{I}\right)} = k$.

For a car travelling north, $\phi = 0$ and so

$$\frac{d^2\theta}{dt^2} + 2k\frac{d\theta}{dt} + k^2\theta = 0.$$

Then $\theta = Ae^{-kt} + Bte^{-kt}$

Initially, $\theta = \theta_0 \Rightarrow A = \theta_0$.

$\dfrac{d\theta}{dt} = 0 \Rightarrow B = k\theta_0$

so $\theta = \theta_0 e^{-kt}(1 + kt)$.

For $0 \le t \le T$, $\quad \dfrac{d^2\theta}{dt^2} + 2k\,\dfrac{d\theta}{dt} + k^2\theta = \dfrac{\pi k}{T}$

$\Rightarrow \theta = Ae^{-kt} + Bte^{-kt} + \dfrac{\pi}{kT}$

Initially, $\theta = 0 \Rightarrow A = -\dfrac{\pi}{kT}$

$\qquad \dfrac{d\theta}{dt} = 0 \Rightarrow B = -\dfrac{\pi}{T}$

For $0 \le t \le T$, $\quad \theta = \dfrac{\pi}{kT}\left(1 - e^{-kt}(1 + kt)\right).$

Then $\dfrac{d\theta}{dt} = \dfrac{\pi k t}{T}\,e^{-kt}$ which is positive for all t.

As $t \to +\infty$, $\theta \to \dfrac{\pi}{kT}$ and so $0 \le \theta \le \dfrac{\pi}{kT}$.

The differential equation is valid for θ such that $\sin\theta \approx \theta$. If $kT > 10\,\pi$, then θ is at most 0.1 radians and $\sin 0.1 = 0.0998$. The solution will therefore be a good approximation to θ.